GOLF CLUBS FOR BEGINNERS

SELECTING, USING, AND IMPROVING YOUR CLUBS

Rico Fairway

Copyright © 2023 Rico Fairway All rights reserved. No part of this publication may be reproduced, stored in or introduced into a retrieval system, or transmitted, in any form, or by any means (electronic, mechanical, photocopying, recording, or otherwise) without the prior written permission of the copyright owner of this book and is illegal and punishable by law.

The information in this book is meant to supplement, not replace, proper golf training. Like any sport involving speed, equipment, balance and environmental factors, golf poses some inherent risk. The authors and publisher advise readers to take full responsibility for their safety and know their limits. Before practicing the skills described in this book, be sure that your equipment is well maintained, and do not take risks beyond your level of experience, aptitude, training, and comfort level.

Download Your Free Gift Now

Discover 17 Simple Tips to IMPROVE Your Golf Game Without Taking a Single Lesson!

As a way of saying "thank you" for your purchase, I'm going to share with you a **Free Gift** exclusive to readers of "Golf Clubs For Beginners."

It will help you master your swing for any given situation on the golf course!

Use the download link **https://bit.ly/3UWNpka** or Scan the barcode to check it out

2

TABLE OF CONTENTS

INTRODUCTION — 5

CHAPTER 1. THE BASICS OF GOLF CLUBS — 9
- The Evolution of Golf Clubs — 11
- Types of Golf Clubs: A Guide for Beginners — 13
- Role and Function of Each Type of Club in Your Game — 15

CHAPTER 2. ANATOMY OF A GOLF CLUB — 17
- Clubhead: Design, Materials, and Their Effects on the Game — 19
- Shaft: Length, Material, and Flex — 22
- Grip: Types, Sizes, and Materials — 24
- How Different Constructions Can Alter the Performance — 26

CHAPTER 3. CHOOSING THE RIGHT CLUBS — 29
- Factors to Consider: Skill Level, Physical Attributes, and Budget — 31
- The Importance of Testing Before Buying — 33
- Purchasing the Right Clubs: New vs. Used — 35

CHAPTER 4. DRIVERS: ANATOMY OF A DRIVER — 37
- Choosing the Right Driver for You — 38
- Techniques and Tips for Using a Driver — 40

CHAPTER 5. IRONS: ANATOMY OF AN IRON — 43
- Types of Irons and Their Uses — 45
- Choosing and Fitting Irons — 46
- Techniques for Different Iron Shots — 48

CHAPTER 6. WEDGES: TYPES OF WEDGES AND THEIR USES — 51
- Wedge Bounce and Grind — 53
- Choosing the Right Wedge — 54
- Techniques for Effective Wedge Play — 56

CHAPTER 7. PUTTERS: TYPES OF PUTTERS — 59
- Choosing the Right Putter — 60
- Fundamentals of Putting — 62
- Advanced Putting Techniques — 63

CHAPTER 8. HYBRIDS: ANATOMY OF A HYBRID — 65
- When to Use a Hybrid — 67
- Choosing the Right Hybrid — 68
- Hybrid Play Techniques — 70

CHAPTER 9. FINE-TUNING YOUR CLUBS — 73
- The Benefits of Club Fitting — 74
- Adjusting Lofts and Lies for Accuracy — 76
- When and Why You Might Need to Re-Grip — 77

CHAPTER 10. GOLF CLUB MAINTENANCE — 81
- Cleaning Routines for Different Clubs — 82
- Proper Storage Tips for Longevity — 84
- Checking for Wear and Tear — 85

CHAPTER 11. THE ART OF THE SWING — 87
- Fundamentals of a Good Golf Swing — 90
- Role of Different Clubs in Swing Mechanics — 91
- Tips to Synchronize Your Swing with Your Clubs — 93

CHAPTER 12. MASTERING THE SHORT GAME — 95
- The Importance of Wedges in Your Short Game — 97
- Chipping, Pitching, and Bunker Play Techniques — 98
- Putting: Choosing the Right Putter and Mastering the Stroke — 100

CHAPTER 13. IMPROVING YOUR GAME — 103
- Practice Routines and Drills — 105
- Using Technology to Analyze and Improve Your Game — 106
- The Importance of Consistent Play with Your Set of Clubs — 108

INTRODUCTION

"Golf is a game of inches. The most important are the six inches between your ears." - Arnold Palmer

Golf, for many, is a beloved pastime, a way to relax and unwind. For others, it's a competitive sport. But for beginners, it can be overwhelming. The sea of golf clubs available, the jargon, and the nuances can be a lot to digest. The good news? You don't need to be a pro to start enjoying this game. All you need is the correct set of golf clubs, guidance, and the will to learn.

Now, choosing the right golf club is crucial. It's not just about the brand or the cost. It's about the feel, the fit, and how it complements your style of play. Remember, the best club in the world will only help if it's right for you. So, where does one start?

The game of golf has a rich history. Traced back to 15th-century Scotland, this sport has evolved significantly. The change is evident from the rudimentary sticks used back then to the technologically advanced clubs of today. And with this evolution, the choices have expanded. For a newbie, this wide array can seem daunting.

However, fear not. This section is here to guide you. We'll explore the basics of selecting the right club. From understanding the different types of clubs to knowing what to look for, we've got you covered. We'll also touch upon using the clubs effectively and ways to improve your game with them.

Golf clubs are extensions of a golfer's arm. They play a pivotal role in the game's outcome. A good club can make the difference between a great shot and a dud. But what makes a club suitable? Is it the material, the design, the weight, or something else?

Material does matter, of course. Modern clubs are made using a variety of materials. There's steel, titanium, and even carbon fiber. Each material has its pros and cons. For instance, steel clubs are durable and provide more control. On the other hand, titanium is lighter and allows for faster swings. Carbon fiber is the latest entrant. It's both lightweight and strong. But there's a catch. It's also pricier.

Design is another critical factor. A club's design can influence its performance. The angle of the clubhead, the groove design, and even the shaft's length play a role. Each design tweak can impact the ball's trajectory, speed, and spin.

Then there's the weight. A heavier club can provide stability. It can also help in delivering powerful shots. But it might only be suitable for some. Some might need help finding them. A lighter club, conversely, can aid in speed. But it might provide a different level of control.

Speaking of control, how you use the club is paramount. The grip, the stance, the swing, and the follow-through - all play a part. A slight misalignment in grip can lead to wayward shots. A wrong stance can affect balance. An incorrect swing can reduce power. And not following through can hamper accuracy.

Improving your game with the club is an ongoing process. It's not just about practicing with the club. It's also about understanding it, knowing its strengths and weaknesses, and adapting your game. And continuously learning and evolving.

For instance, if you've chosen a steel club, understand its weight. Use it to your advantage. Deliver powerful shots where needed. If it's a titanium one, leverage its speed.

Deliver fast swings to cover more ground. And if it's carbon fiber, strike a balance. Use its strength and lightness judiciously.

But remember, no club is perfect. Each will have its quirks. The key is to adapt. Learn from each shot. Understand what went wrong or right. And then adjust. Over time, you'll not only get better with the club but also at the game.

In the end, golf is not just about the clubs. It's also about the golfer. The clubs are tools. They aid in the game. But it's the golfer who makes the real difference. The skills, mindset, and determination all play a part.

So, as you venture into the world of golf, remember this. The right club can help. But your passion, dedication, and will to improve will take you far. Whether it's the lush greens of Pebble Beach or your local golf course, the journey will be rewarding. And with the right club in hand, the game will be even more enjoyable.

CHAPTER 1.
THE BASICS OF GOLF CLUBS

"Golf is a game in which you yell 'fore,' shoot six, and write down five." - Paul Harvey

Welcome to the world of golf, a game that's not just about swinging and scoring but also about the art of choosing the right club. Your club is your companion on the field, the tool that turns your strategies into reality. Understanding the basics of golf clubs is your first step toward mastering this beautiful game.

Before we dive into the types of clubs, let's talk about the club's anatomy. Each club comprises three parts: the grip, the shaft, and the clubhead. Each part plays a crucial role in the game. The grip is where you hold the club, designed to provide comfort and control. The shaft connects the grip to the clubhead, affecting the club's flexibility. The clubhead is where the magic happens; it's the part that hits the ball.

There are primarily five types of clubs: drivers, fairway woods, hybrids, irons, and putters. Each one is designed for a specific purpose and used under different circumstances. With its oversized clubhead and long shaft, a driver is used for distance. You'll most likely use it for your first shot on most holes. Fairway woods are versatile, designed for long shots on the fairway and sometimes for tee shots on short holes.

Hybrids are the new kids on the block. As the name suggests, they combine the characteristics of woods and irons. They're easier to hit than long irons and used for shots requiring more control. Irons come in various designs, ranging from 1-iron to 9-iron, with the number indicating the clubhead's loft. The higher the number, the higher the loft, and the shorter the distance. Finally, the putter, your best friend on the green, is used for short and low-speed strokes.

Choosing the right club at the right time is an art. It depends on the distance to the hole, the terrain, and your comfort. For instance, if you're 150 yards from the hole, you might reach for your 7-iron. But if there's a water hazard in the way, or the wind blows against you, a 6-iron or even a 5-iron might be better.

Club fitting is an essential aspect of the game. A club that's too long, short, heavy, or light can affect your swing and overall performance. It's not just about your height; your swing speed, stance, and even your grip size play a role in determining the right club for you. Therefore, consider getting a professional club fitting before buying your first set of clubs.

Now, let's talk about fairway woods. These clubs are designed to hit the ball long distances from the fairway. They have a smaller clubhead than drivers but a larger one than irons. The more oversized clubhead provides more forgiveness, making it easier to hit the ball properly. The most common fairway woods are the 3-wood and 5-wood, named based on their loft.

The 3-wood, also known as a fairway driver, usually has a loft between 12 and 17 degrees, ideal for long-distance shots. The 5-wood, a loft between 20 and 23 degrees, is a versatile club often used for shorter, more controlled shots.

However, the choice between a 3-wood and a 5-wood, or any other club, is still being determined. It depends on the situation and your comfort level.

Some golfers prefer a 5-wood for a particular shot, while others choose a 3-wood. The key is experimenting with different clubs and finding the ones that suit your style and situation.

The Evolution of Golf Clubs

"A good golfer has the determination to win and the patience to wait for the breaks." - Gary Player

Once upon a time, golfers didn't have the luxury of modern clubs. They played with wooden sticks. Golf clubs have come a long way from their humble beginnings. Let's take a trip back in time and understand the evolution of golf clubs.

Golf was born in Scotland during the Middle Ages. The early clubs were wooden sticks, often carved personally by the golfers. These rudimentary clubs were made from various woods, like ash and beech. They were adequate for the time but needed more precision and durability.

Through the 17th and 18th centuries, the crafting of golf clubs became a trade. Clubmakers used different woods for the shaft and the clubhead. Hickory, known for its strength and flexibility, was the preferred shaft choice. On the other hand, clubheads were made from tougher woods like beech, apple, and pear.

The 19th century saw the introduction of iron clubs. Blacksmiths usually forged these clubs. Iron clubs offered more durability and control but were still relatively crude compared to today's clubs.

The introduction of the Haskell ball in the early 20th century marked a turning point. This new kind of golf ball, made with rubber, was more resilient and could be hit further. This required clubs with greater precision. Clubmakers started using steel shafts, which were stronger and more consistent than hickory.

It was around this time that the numbering system for clubs was introduced. Before this, clubs had colorful names like "Mashie" and "Niblick". The introduction of numbers made it easier to identify the function of each club.

The second half of the 20th century saw more innovations. The use of synthetic materials, like plastic and graphite, became common. These materials were lighter and allowed for faster swing speeds. Also, perimeter weighting was introduced to make clubs more forgiving on off-center hits.

The 21st century has seen further advances. Modern technology has allowed for the design of clubs that maximize power and control. Computer simulations and advanced materials have led to clubs that can be finely tuned to the needs of individual golfers.

Today, golf clubs are meticulously designed. Clubmakers consider factors like swing speed, launch angle, and spin rate. The result is a range of clubs that cater to golfers of all skill levels.

Getting a proper club fitting is essential. This ensures that your clubs match your physical attributes and skill level. It can make a significant difference to your game.

Each club in your bag has a specific purpose. The driver, the longest club, is used for maximum distance off the tee. Fairway woods are used for long shots from the fairway. Irons are used for various shots, from the tee, fairway, or rough. Wedges are used for short shots and chips around the green. And the putter, of course, is used on the green.

Knowing when and why to use each club is vital to golf strategy. This understanding comes with experience and practice. So pick up your clubs and hit the course. The world of golf awaits you.

Let's remember the golf club's visual appeal. Golf clubs have become more aesthetically pleasing over the years. Today's sleek and stylish clubs add to the game's allure.

Types of Golf Clubs: A Guide for Beginners

"Golf is a compromise between what your ego wants you to do, what experience tells you to do, and what your nerves let you do." - Bruce Crampton

Each golf club is designed for a specific purpose, and using the right one can drastically improve your game. This section will explore drivers, irons, wedges, putters, and hybrids.

Drivers

A driver is the longest club in a golfer's bag. It's designed to hit the ball the farthest. A driver is typically used for the first shot on a par 4 or par 5 hole. The driver's large head and long shaft are engineered for maximum distance. This club is challenging to master, but you can make impressive tee shots with practice.

Irons

Irons are versatile clubs in different sizes, from 1-iron to 9-iron. The lower the number, the longer the shaft, and the less loft the club has. A 1-iron will hit the ball further but with a lower trajectory than a 9-iron. Irons are typically used for shots on the fairway and approaches to the green.

Wedges

Wedges are a subtype of irons with a higher loft, used for short-distance shots. These clubs are perfect for getting your ball out of tricky spots like bunkers and thick rough. There are four types of wedges: pitching wedge, gap wedge, sand wedge, and lob wedge. Each wedge has a specific loft and bounce designed for different situations on the golf course.

Putters

A putter is a club that makes short, low-speed strokes to roll the ball into the hole. It's used on the green, the area around the hole, where precision is critical. Putters come in various sizes and designs, but they all serve the same purpose - to get the ball into the hole with the least number of strokes.

Hybrids

Hybrid golf clubs are a cross between fairway woods and irons, combining the best features of both. They are designed to be easier to hit than long irons and provide more distance than high-lofted woods. Hybrids are an excellent option for beginners who find long irons challenging to hit.

Now that we've covered the basics of the different types of golf clubs, you're one step closer to understanding the game. Remember, a good golfer must do more than hit the ball far. It's about knowing when to use which club, understanding the course, and playing strategically.

But how do you know which clubs are right for you? Getting a proper club fitting before purchasing is essential. As you progress with your game, you may prefer certain clubs over others. That's perfectly okay.

The most important thing is to practice. Practice with different clubs and in various situations. Over time, you'll gain experience and confidence. Remember the quote we started with? "Golf is a compromise between what your ego wants you to do, what experience tells you to do, and what your nerves let you do." So listen to your experience and learn from it.

Role and Function of Each Type of Club in Your Game

As a beginner, understanding the game of golf can feel like learning a new language. But fear not because, just like any language, everything else falls into place once you grasp the basics. We will break down the roles and functions of different golf clubs, simplifying the process and making golf more enjoyable for you.

Let's start with the driver. The driver is the longest club in your bag, and it's designed for tee shots on long holes. It's the club you'll use to start most holes, and it's built to send the ball flying towards the fairway. Golf drivers have the lowest loft, which means they're designed to hit the ball a long distance.

Next, we have fairway woods. You can use These versatile clubs for long shots from the fairway or even off the tee when the driver might be too much club. Fairway Woods can also be used for recovery shots when trying to regain position after an errant shot.

Hybrids are a relatively new addition to the golf club family. They combine the best features of woods and irons. Because of their more forgiving design, beginners often find hybrids easier to hit than long irons. They can be used from the fairway, rough, and even off the tee in certain situations.

Irons are used for a variety of shots on the golf course. They range from long irons (2-4), which are used for long distances, to middle irons (5-7) for mid-range shots and short irons (8-9) for closer shots. The higher the iron number, the higher the loft, which means the ball will fly higher and shorter.

Wedges are specialized irons used for short shots near the green and for getting out of tough spots like sand bunkers. They have the highest loft of any club, which helps to lift the ball into the air and stop quickly on the green.

Last but not least, the putter. The putter is the club you'll use most often. It plays an essential role in scoring and is used to roll the ball on the green towards the hole. While it might not seem as thrilling as smashing a driver, developing a good putting stroke can significantly improve your scores.

Now that we've broken down the different types of clubs, let's remember that each has a unique role. The key is to understand when and why to use each club, depending on the shot you face. This requires practice and experience, but don't worry; with time and patience, you'll become more comfortable and confident in deciding which club is right for each shot.

Proper club fitting is advisable in the early stages of your golf journey. This will ensure your clubs are tailored to your physical characteristics and swing style. Playing with clubs that aren't right for you can impede your progress and make the game more challenging than it needs to be.

In conclusion, understanding the ins and outs of your golf clubs is a crucial step in learning the game. Each club serves a different purpose, and knowing when to use each will help you navigate the golf course and improve your scores. Remember, golf is a game of patience and precision, not power and speed. So, take your time, practice regularly, and, most importantly, enjoy the journey.

Now that you better understand the role and function of each type of club in your game, it's time to hit the course and put your knowledge into practice. Remember, the most important golf shot is the next one, so focus on each shot one at a time, and before you know it, you'll be playing with confidence and enjoying this great game even more.

CHAPTER 2.
ANATOMY OF A GOLF CLUB

Understanding your golf club as a beginner is much like getting to know a new friend. You'll learn about its parts and functions and how it can help you improve your game. The first step is to understand the anatomy of a golf club.

A golf club has three main parts: the grip, the shaft, and the head. The grip is the part of the club that you hold. It's usually made of rubber or leather, and its purpose is to provide a firm hold without slipping. The grip quality can significantly influence your swing, so it's crucial to ensure it's comfortable and fits well in your hands.

The shaft is the long, slender part of the club that connects the grip to the head. It's typically made from steel or graphite, with each material offering different benefits. Steel shafts are more durable and less expensive but heavier. Graphite shafts are lighter and can help increase swing speed, but they're more expensive.

The head of the club is the part that hits the ball. It has several components, including the face, the hosel, and the sole. The face is the flat area that strikes the ball. The grooves on the face help control the ball's spin and direction.

The hosel is where the shaft of the club connects to the head. It plays a crucial role in determining the club's lie angle, which is the angle between the shaft and the ground when the club is in a proper address position.

The club's sole is the bottom part that rests on the ground. It's designed to slide over the turf when you swing, minimizing the chances of digging into the ground.

Understanding these parts and how they work together can help you select the right club for your game. For example, a club with a stiffer shaft may be beneficial if you have a fast swing speed. A club with a larger head is a good choice if you hit the ball with the club's toe or heel.

Getting a proper club fitting is an essential step before purchasing your golf clubs. A club fitting involves measuring your swing speed, ball speed, and launch angle to determine the best clubs for your game. It can also include evaluating your physical characteristics, such as height and arm length, to ensure the clubs are the correct length for you.

Different clubs are used for different situations in a game of golf. The driver, the largest club, is used for long-distance shots typically taken from the tee. Fairway woods are used for long shots from the fairway. In contrast, hybrids, a combination of woods and irons, are versatile and can be used for various shots. Irons are used for shorter shots, and wedges for short shots and shots from the sand. The putter is used on the green for rolling the ball into the hole.

Understanding the anatomy of a golf club and when and why to use particular clubs can help improve your game. It can help you make more informed decisions about which club to use in different situations. It can lead to more consistent and accurate shots.

The next part of your golf journey involves practice. Familiarize yourself with your clubs, get comfortable with your grip and stance, and spend time on the driving range.

Remember, every golfer was once a beginner. You'll see improvement in your game with patience, persistence, and a solid understanding of your golf clubs.

Remember what Jack Nicklaus, one of the greatest golfers of all time, once said: "Don't be too proud to take a lesson. I'm not."

Clubhead: Design, Materials, and Their Effects on the Game

"Give me a lever long enough and a fulcrum on which to place it, and I shall move the world." — Archimedes

This quote is, in essence, about how tools are designed and used. In golf, the clubhead is the 'lever' that can move the 'world' of a golf ball.

The design of the clubhead carries a lot of weight in the game of golf. It's not just about the look or feel. The shape, size, and material can significantly impact the swing, ball flight, and overall shot results. The clubhead is designed to connect with the ball, and how it's made can make a massive difference in your game.

Fig. 42

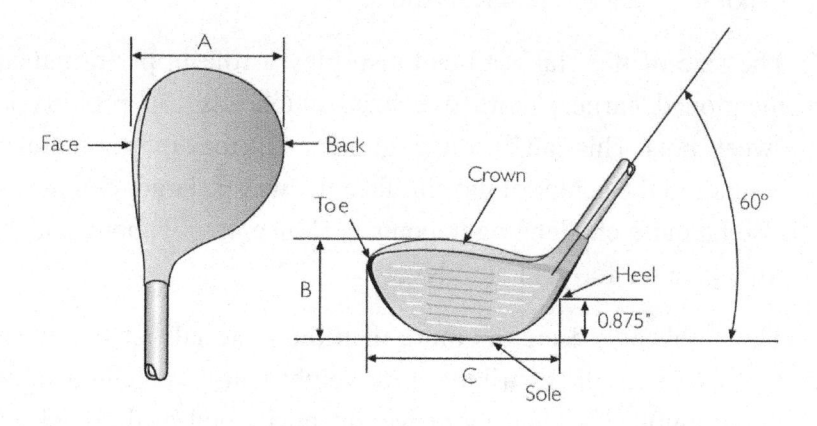

The clubhead's material is a significant factor that affects the performance of a club. Traditionally, woods were made from actual hardwood trees like persimmon.

These days, clubheads are typically made from metal alloys, such as titanium or steel. The weight and strength of these materials enable longer and more accurate shots.

Titanium is a popular choice for drivers because it's lightweight yet strong. It allows for larger clubhead sizes without increasing the club's overall weight. A more oversized clubhead can provide a larger sweet spot, the area on the clubface that delivers the most distance when appropriately struck. Larger clubhead sizes can be a great advantage for beginners still improving their aim.

On the other hand, steel is used more in irons and putters. It's heavier than titanium, which can provide more control in the short game. The steel weight can help you feel the swing more, improving your swing mechanics and consistency.

Now, let's discuss the shape and size of the clubhead. The shape can affect how the club interacts with the ball and the turf. For instance, a clubhead with a flat leading edge can help reduce turf interference, making it easier to hit clean shots.

The size of the clubhead can also play a role in performance. As mentioned earlier, more oversized clubheads can provide larger sweet spots. This can benefit beginners who may only sometimes hit the ball in the center of the clubface. However, larger clubheads can also be more challenging to control. Hence, it's all about finding the right balance for your skill level.

The clubhead's design is more than the materials, size, and shape. It's also about the distribution of weight within the clubhead itself. Some clubheads have more weight positioned at the back or the perimeter.

This helps increase the moment of inertia, which means the club is more resistant to twisting on off-center hits. This can lead to straighter shots, even when the ball isn't struck perfectly.

The grooves on the clubface also play a significant role. They provide spin and control on the ball, allowing it to fly in the desired direction and stop quicker on the greens. Different clubs have groove designs in a golfer's bag to suit their roles.

So, you see, the clubhead design and material significantly affect the game. It's not just about picking a club that looks good. Understanding the science behind the clubhead can dramatically improve your game, especially if you're starting.

Remember, golf is a game of skill and precision. The right clubhead can be your best ally on the course, helping you hit longer, straighter, and more accurate shots. So, take the time to understand the clubhead's design and materials and see how it can improve your game.

It might seem complex at first, but once you start seeing the results on the course, you'll understand the importance of the clubhead's design and materials. So, consider these factors whether you're choosing your first set of clubs or looking to upgrade. You'll improve your game and increase your understanding and appreciation of this wonderful sport. Golf isn't just a game of physical skill but also a game of knowledge and understanding.

As in life, the right tools can make all the difference in golf. The clubhead is one such tool; understanding its design and materials can significantly improve your game. So, don't just pick up any club. Choose wisely, understand how it works, and see the difference it can make in your game. This knowledge will improve your shots and enhance your overall golfing experience.

Just as Archimedes said, give him a lever and a place to stand, and he could move the world. In golf, the right clubhead can move the world of your game. So, choose wisely and play well.

Shaft: Length, Material, and Flex

Golf is a good walk spoiled. - Mark Twain

Welcome to the exciting world of golf! As a beginner, there's quite a bit to learn, from the game's rules to the types of clubs. For the moment, let's focus on an essential part of your golf club: the shaft. The shaft of a golf club plays a crucial role in your swing's performance and affects the distance and accuracy of your shots.

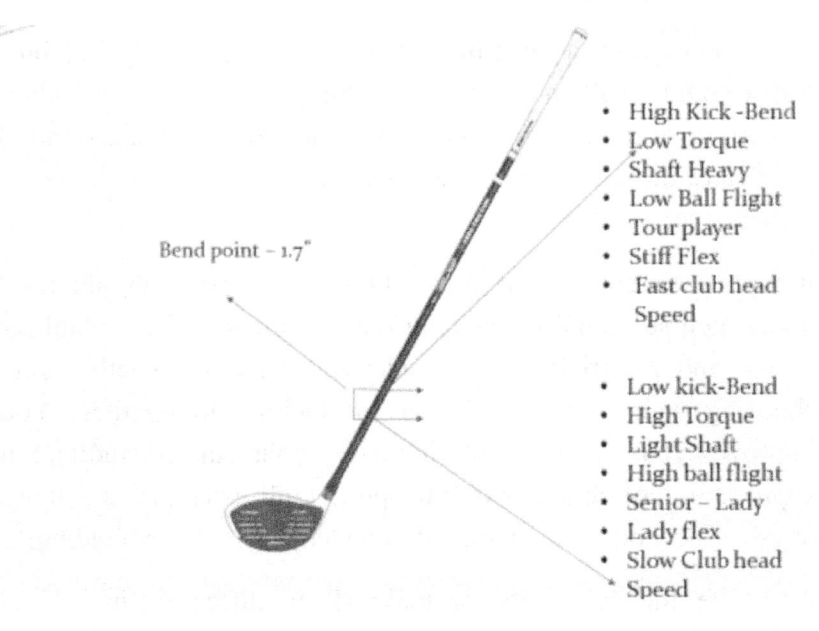

Bend point - 1.7"

- High Kick - Bend
- Low Torque
- Shaft Heavy
- Low Ball Flight
- Tour player
- Stiff Flex
- Fast club head Speed

- Low kick - Bend
- High Torque
- Light Shaft
- High ball flight
- Senior – Lady
- Lady flex
- Slow Club head Speed

The first thing you need to know about the shaft is its length. The shaft length can significantly affect the control and distance of your swing. Choosing the correct length for your height and swing style is essential. For instance, taller golfers often benefit from longer shafts, while shorter golfers might find shorter shafts more comfortable. There's no one-size-fits-all approach here—you'll need to find what works best for your needs.

A common misconception among beginners is that a longer shaft will automatically result in longer drives. While it's true that a longer shaft can increase swing speed, it can also lead to less control and accuracy. So, don't be tempted to choose the longest shaft in hopes of becoming the next long-drive champion. Instead, focus on finding a length that allows you to hit the sweet spot on the clubface consistently.

Next, let's talk about the material of the shaft. The two most common types of shaft materials are steel and graphite. Each material has its pros and cons and can significantly impact your game.

Steel shafts are typically heavier and offer more control, making them popular among professional golfers. They're also more durable and generally less expensive than graphite shafts. However, the increased weight might make them less suitable for golfers with slower swing speeds.

On the other hand, graphite shafts are lighter and can help increase swing speed, potentially leading to longer distances. They're also better at absorbing the vibrations caused by impact, which can reduce the strain on your hands and arms. However, this comes at the cost of less control and a higher price tag compared to steel shafts.

Lastly, let's delve into the flex of the shaft. The flex refers to how much the shaft bends when force is applied during the swing. There are five main categories of shaft flex: Extra Stiff (X), Stiff (S), Regular (R), Senior (A), and Ladies (L).

The type of flex shaft you need depends on your swing speed. Golfers with faster swing speeds typically benefit from stiffer shafts. In contrast, those with slower swing speeds find more flexible shafts beneficial. A shaft that's too stiff for your swing speed can lead to shots that are low and to the right, while a too flexible shaft can lead to high shots and to the left.

Grip: Types, Sizes, and Materials

Golf, my friend, is indeed a game of subtleties. One subtlety that beginners often overlook is the grip on your golf club. It's more than just an add-on to your club; it's a crucial part of the tool that connects you to your game. Let's dive into this vital aspect of golf - the grip.

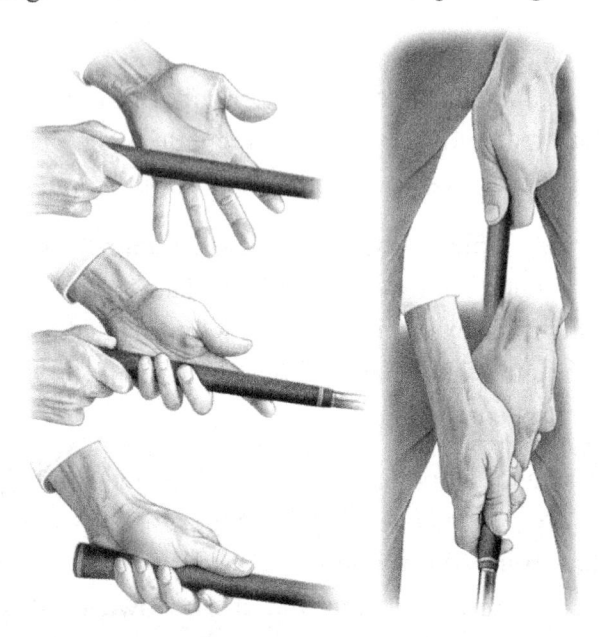

When you first pick up a golf club, the grip is what you feel. It must be suitable for your hand size and comfortable for your hold. A grip that's too large can lead to a lack of control, while a grip that's too small can cause you to overcompensate and distort your swing. Therefore, size is a considerable factor when it comes to grips.

There are typically three grip sizes: standard, midsize, and jumbo. The standard grip fits most golfers. However, if you have larger hands or are gripping the club too hard, a midsize or jumbo grip might suit you better.

Then, there's the matter of grip type. The most common types are rubber and corded grips. Rubber grips are favored by many due to their durability and wide range of texture options.

On the other hand, corded grips offer excellent traction, making them perfect for golfers who play in wet weather or have sweaty hands.

The material of your grip also plays a significant role in your comfort and control. Rubber is the most common material in golf grips due to its durability and versatility. It can be molded into various shapes and textures, giving you multiple options to fit your preferences.

Cord grips often combine rubber with cotton fibers to give a rougher texture, enhancing the grip even in wet conditions. Once a popular choice for grips, leather offers a soft and tacky feel but requires more upkeep than rubber or cord grips.

Another material that has gained popularity is synthetic polymers, known for their durability and wide range of textures and firmness. These materials can be designed to have a soft, tacky feel, resembling that of a leather grip or a firm, durable feel like a rubber grip.

But choosing a grip isn't merely about picking a size, type, and material you like. It's about understanding how these factors can affect your game. For instance, a larger grip can help reduce the pressure on your hands and promote a smoother swing. However, it may limit your hand action, leading to a tendency to leave the clubface open at impact, pushing the shot to the right.

On the other hand, a smaller grip may enhance your hand action, which can help correct a slice by enabling the clubface to close more easily at impact. But, it may also cause you to grip the club too tightly, leading to tension in your hands and forearms, potentially disrupting your swing.

The type and material of your grip can affect your feel of the club and your level of traction. A grip with a rougher texture or a corded grip can offer better traction, ensuring the club doesn't slip in your hands. However, they may also be more demanding on your hands, especially if you golf without gloves.

A smoother texture or a rubber grip may be more comfortable. Still, it might provide a different level of traction, especially in wet conditions. You might also find that different materials wear down at different rates, affecting the lifespan of your grip.

Ultimately, selecting the right grip comes down to personal comfort and how it can enhance your swing mechanics. It's about finding the balance between comfort, control, and consistency. So, pay attention to this crucial aspect of your golf equipment. As the great Arnold Palmer once said, golf is a game of inches. And the grip on your club plays a significant role in controlling those inches.

Remember, it's not just about having the right clubs; it's about having the proper grip on them. So, take the time to understand golf grips' types, sizes, and materials. Test different ones to see what works best for you and your game. After all, golf is a game of subtleties, and minor adjustments can make the most significant difference.

How Different Constructions Can Alter the Performance

"Success in golf depends less on strength of body than on the strength of mind and character." - Arnold Palmer

Just as the strength of mind and character can influence your game, how your golf clubs are constructed can significantly impact your performance on the golf course. Specifically for beginners, understanding the role of different constructions in golf clubs is crucial for enhancing your gameplay.

Like any other sports equipment, golf clubs are designed with meticulous attention to detail. Each golf club component, from its head to the grip, can alter how you swing and hit the ball. For instance, the weight distribution in a club's head can influence the trajectory and distance of your shots.

Consider the clubhead. It's the part that contacts the ball, so its construction significantly impacts your shot. A more oversized clubhead offers a bigger "sweet spot," which can be forgiving for beginners, leading to less drastic effects on off-center hits. Meanwhile, a smaller clubhead can provide more experienced players with greater control and precision.

Another crucial component is the golf club shaft, which connects the grip to the club head. It comes in different materials, lengths, and flexes. A shorter shaft can provide better control, while a longer one can generate more distance. Similarly, a stiffer shaft flex suits golfers with a faster swing speed, while a more flexible shaft is better for slower swingers.

Now, take a look at the grip. It's your only contact point with the club, and its size and texture can significantly affect your swing. A too-large grip can limit wrist action, leading to a slice, while a too-small grip can cause the club to twist, leading to a hook.

The loft, or the angle of the clubface, also plays a vital role. A higher loft angle can help lift the ball into the air, which is ideal for beginners who struggle with getting the ball airborne. On the other hand, a lower loft can lead to longer shots but requires more skill to hit accurately.

The lie angle, the angle between the center of the shaft and the sole of the club, is another critical factor. An incorrect lie angle can cause the clubface to be misaligned at impact, leading to inaccurate shots.

When it comes to golf club construction, even the smallest details matter. The type of material used, the design features, and how they're assembled can significantly impact your performance. For instance, clubs made from titanium are lighter, allowing for more incredible swing speed and distance. However, they might provide a different level of control than clubs made from heavier materials like steel.

Choosing the right golf club involves more than picking the shiniest or most expensive one off the shelf. It's about understanding how different constructions can alter your performance and finding the balance that suits your swing and playing style.

Remember, golf is a game of precision and control. The right golf club can help you achieve that, but practicing and improving your technique is essential. After all, even the best golf club can't substitute for skill and experience.

By understanding the impact of different constructions on golf club performance, you'll be better equipped to choose and use the right clubs effectively. Whether it's a driver, fairway wood, iron, wedge, or putter, each club has its unique construction and purpose in your golf bag.

As a beginner, take your time with the complexities of golf club construction. Start with a basic set of clubs, understand their construction and how it impacts their performance, and gradually upgrade as your skills improve.

Ultimately, it's about more than having the best golf clubs but how well you use them. That starts with understanding how different constructions can alter the performance so you can make informed choices and play a better game of golf.

CHAPTER 3.
CHOOSING THE RIGHT CLUBS

Choosing the right clubs can feel like a puzzle when starting in golf. But don't worry. This chapter will help you solve it.

Clubs are the tools of the trade in golf. They're your weapons on the battlefield. But not all clubs are created equal. Some are designed for distance, some for accuracy, and some for specific situations on the golf course. Understanding their differences and knowing when to use each can drastically improve your game.

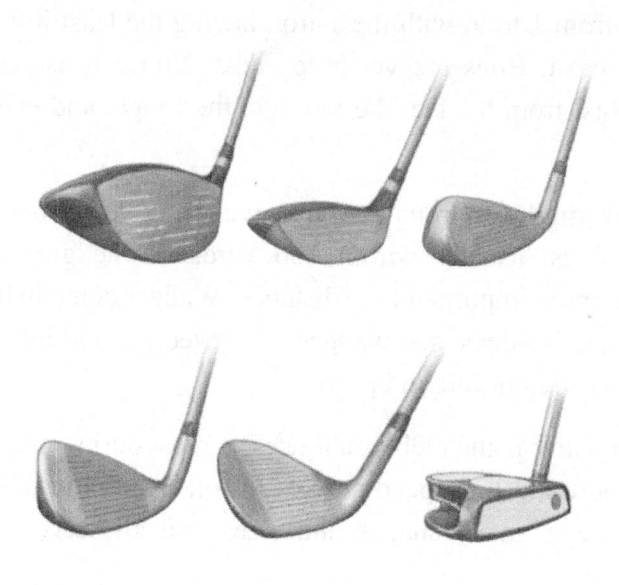

Let's start with the basics. A standard golf set includes woods, irons, wedges, and a putter. Woods are for distance, irons for control, wedges for close shots, and the putter for that final, crucial shot into the hole. You can carry up to 14 clubs in your bag during a round, but you only need so many as a beginner. A driver, a fairway wood, a few irons, a wedge, and a putter will suffice.

The driver, known as the 1-wood, is the longest club in the bag and can send the ball the farthest. It's the club you'll usually use to tee off on par 4 and par 5 holes. But the driver is also one of the most challenging clubs to master. Its long shaft and low loft make it challenging to control, especially for beginners.

Fairway woods, numbered from 3 to 7, are shorter and easier to handle than the driver. They're great for long shots from the fairway, hence the name. The higher the number, the shorter the club and the higher its loft, which means it will send the ball higher and a shorter distance.

Irons are even shorter and have even more loft than woods. They're numbered from 1 to 9, with the 1-iron having the least loft and the 9-iron the most. Irons are versatile clubs. You can use them for various shots, from the tee, the fairway, the rough, and even some hazards.

Wedges are similar to irons but have even more loft. They're used for short shots, usually within 100 yards of the green, where precision is more important than distance. Wedges come in different types: pitching wedges, gap wedges, sand wedges, and lob wedges, each with a different loft and purpose.

Lastly, the putter is the club you'll use the most during a round. It's used for short and low-speed strokes to roll the ball into the hole. Putters come in many shapes and sizes, but all serve the same purpose.

Choosing the right clubs is one thing, but using them correctly is another. That's where club fitting comes in. Club fitting is the process of adjusting the clubs to fit your swing. A proper club fitting can make a big difference in your game. It can help you hit the ball farther, straighter, and more consistently.

Getting a club fitting before purchasing your clubs is a good idea. It might sound intimidating, especially if you're new to golf, but don't be. Club fitting isn't just for pros. Beginners might benefit from it the most. A club fitting can help you understand your swing and identify the clubs that suit you best.

Remember, the right clubs depend on your skills and characteristics rather than what your favorite golfer uses or is advertised as the latest and greatest. What matters most is that the clubs fit you and your game.

Choosing the right clubs and using them correctly can give you a solid foundation. But improving your game continues beyond there. Practice is key. The more you play, the better you'll understand your clubs and how to use them in different situations.

Golf is a game of skill, patience, and strategy. But it's also a game of tools. The right clubs can make a huge difference. Choose wisely, use properly, and always strive to improve. Your game will thank you.

Factors to Consider: Skill Level, Physical Attributes, and Budget

"Beware of the man who works hard to learn something, learns it, and finds himself no wiser than before." Kurt Vonnegut once shared this insight. As you embark on your golfing adventure, the wisdom in these words rings true.

The game of golf is not merely about mastering the swing or understanding the course. It's also about choosing the right equipment. One of the essential pieces of equipment you will need is the golf club. Selecting the appropriate golf club can be daunting, especially for a beginner. However, consider three key factors: your skill level, physical attributes, and budget.

As a beginner, your skill level is crucial to your club selection. You want to avoid picking a club designed for seasoned players. Such clubs often require precise control and technique, which you must still develop. Instead, opt for clubs that offer forgiveness on off-center hits, which will more accommodate your developing skill level.

Your physical attributes also play a significant role in club selection. This refers to your height, strength, and the speed of your swing. Golf clubs come in different sizes, and using one that's too long or too short can affect your swing. Similarly, if the club is too heavy, it can slow down your swing speed, reducing the distance of your shots. A proper club fitting before purchasing can help you find the right club for your physical attributes.

Your budget is another essential factor to consider. Golf clubs can range from affordable to extremely expensive, with prices often reflecting the materials used and the technology incorporated. As a beginner, you don't need the most expensive club. Instead, look for one that suits your skill level and physical attributes, and fits within your budget.

In golf, the fairway wood is an important club to have in your bag. This club is designed for long-distance shots from the fairway and tee shots on long par-3 holes. The fairway wood's design, with a larger head and a long shaft, allows for greater distance with less effort. As a beginner, having a fairway wood in your bag can make the game more enjoyable as you develop your skills.

Understanding when and why to use specific clubs is another critical game aspect. Each club has a particular purpose and is designed for specific situations. For example, you would use a driver for long-distance tee shots, a wedge for short-distance shots, and a putter for putting on the green. By understanding the purpose of each club, you can make better decisions on the course.

Images of golf clubs can also help you understand the differences between them. The photos show different clubs' designs, sizes, and shape variations. This can provide a visual guide as you learn about the different types of golf clubs and their uses.

The Importance of Testing Before Buying

You can't learn to swim by reading about the water. You have to jump in. The same principle holds for golf. As a beginner, you could be eager to buy your first set of golf clubs. But hold on! Here's a crucial piece of advice - always test before buying.

Getting the right golf clubs is like finding the perfect pair of shoes. If you try them on first, you'll select what's comfortable over how they look. The same applies to golf clubs. When you hold a club, it should feel like an extension of your body. It should be comfortable, the weight should feel right, and you should be able to swing it easily.

Golf is a game of precision and control. Each club in your golf bag has a specific purpose and is designed for a particular type of shot. The driver, for example, is meant for the longest shots. On the other hand, the putter is designed for short, precise shots on the green.

You might be tempted to buy a complete set of clubs as a beginner. However, think about this - do you need all those clubs? Each club has a different loft, length, and weight. As a beginner, you must gain the skills to use them effectively.

Instead of buying a complete set, consider starting with a few essential clubs - a driver, a fairway wood, a few irons, and a putter. These clubs will cover most of the shots you must make on the golf course. You can add more clubs to your bag as you gain more experience and improve your skills.

Now, you might wonder where to test golf clubs before buying them. Most golf retailers and pro shops offer demo days where you can try out different clubs. These events are an excellent opportunity to test various clubs and find the ones that suit your swing and style of play.

Another option is to get a club fitting. During a club fitting, a professional club fitter will assess your swing and recommend clubs that match your swing speed, style, and physical characteristics. A proper club fitting can make a significant difference in your game. It can improve your accuracy, distance, and overall performance on the golf course.

When testing golf clubs, pay attention to how the club feels in your hands. The grip should be comfortable, and the club should feel light enough. Also, observe how the club performs. Are you able to hit the ball straight and far? Is the ball trajectory consistent? These are crucial factors to consider when choosing golf clubs.

Remember, golf clubs are not one-size-fits-all. What works for one golfer might not work for another. Therefore, it's essential to test different clubs and find the ones that suit you best. Don't rush the process. Take your time, try various clubs, and choose the ones that enhance your game.

Purchasing the Right Clubs: New vs. Used

"Golf is a game of respect, and respect begins with the tools of the trade."

Golf is a captivating sport, but the tools of the game can truly make or break your experience. One of the key tools you'll need as you begin your golfing adventure is your golf clubs. The question that arises for many new golfers is, "Should I buy new or used clubs?"

There's no easy answer because it all depends on your needs, budget, and goals in the game. Let's start by discussing the pros and cons of new and used clubs; then, you can make an informed decision that suits you best.

When you're just starting, new clubs can be tempting. They're shiny, untouched, and often come with the latest technology. They promise optimal performance and have a certain appeal to them. Plus, they're yours and yours alone from the get-go, which can add to the personal attachment you might feel to the game.

One of the most significant benefits of new clubs is that they can be custom-fitted to your specific needs. A proper club fitting ensures that your clubs match your swing style, physique, and skill level. This can be crucial for your development as a golfer. Clubs that are too long, short, heavy, or light can lead to bad habits and hinder your progress.

On the other hand, new clubs are expensive. Suppose golf is a long-term commitment for you. In that case, there may be better ideas than investing significant money into brand-new clubs. And while the latest technology can help improve your game, as a beginner, the nuances of such technology might make a slight difference to your game later.

Now, let's talk about used clubs. They are a popular choice among beginners for many reasons, the most obvious being cost. Used clubs are significantly cheaper than new ones, making golf a much more accessible sport for many people. It can be economical to get started without a huge financial commitment.

Used clubs also have the advantage of having been 'broken in.' This means that any manufacturing quirks have likely been worn away, and the clubs are ready for smooth operation. You also have the opportunity to try out different clubs and see which ones work best for you without breaking the bank.

There are, however, some risks involved with buying used clubs. They may have hidden damages that could affect their performance. Additionally, they might fit you differently, as they were initially tailored for someone else. While you can have used clubs refitted, it's only sometimes possible to achieve the perfect fit.

CHAPTER 4.

DRIVERS: ANATOMY OF A DRIVER

The first part of the driver we need to understand is the clubhead. The clubhead is the part of the driver that hits the ball. For maximum durability and optimum performance, it's typically made of metals, including titanium and steel.

Next up, we have the loft. The loft refers to the angle of the clubface that controls trajectory. Essentially, the loft is responsible for how high and far the ball will go when you hit it. A higher loft is usually recommended for beginners because it helps hit the ball higher into the air and cover more distance.

Now, let's talk about the shaft. The shaft of a golf driver is just as important as the clubhead. It's like the engine that powers the club, transferring the energy from your swing to the ball. The shaft comes in various materials, including steel and graphite. As a beginner golfer, opt for a graphite shaft as it tends to be lighter and can help you swing faster.

Following the shaft, we have the grip. The grip is where you hold the driver. A good grip on your driver ensures control over your swing. Most golf drivers come with grips made from rubber or synthetic materials, offering a comfortable hold and better control.

Next, we have the hosel. The hosel is where the driver's shaft connects with the clubhead. It's crucial as it can affect the alignment of the club. Some drivers feature adjustable hosels, which allow you to change the club's loft and lie angle.

And lastly, we have the face of the driver. The face is the part of the clubhead that makes contact with the ball. The design of the face can influence how the ball behaves upon impact. Some drivers feature a larger face, which can be more forgiving on off-center hits.

Now that we have a basic understanding of the parts of a driver let's talk about how they work together. When you swing the driver, the shaft flexes and stores energy. This energy is released as you come down on your swing, propelling the ball forward.

The driver's loft determines the ball's initial direction, while the driver's face influences the spin. The more spin a ball has, the higher and farther it will go. However, too much spin can cause the ball to veer off course.

The grip and the hosel play a vital role in controlling your swing. A good grip ensures control over the club, while the hosel's position can affect the club's alignment and loft.

Choosing the Right Driver for You

"The perfect driver is the one that you hit straightest most often." - Jack Nicklaus

The tools you use can make or break your efforts in any walk of life. The game of golf is no different. The trick is to choose the perfect driver for you. A driver is one of the most important clubs in a golfer's bag. It's used for long-distance shots, usually off the tee.

To choose the right driver, you must first understand what a driver is. It's the longest club in your bag and has the largest head.

The size of the driver's head is crucial because it provides a large hitting area. This can help you make solid contact with the ball, even if your swing isn't perfect.

The loft of your driver also matters. The loft is the angle of the clubface that controls trajectory and affects distance. A higher loft will launch the ball higher into the air. A lower loft will make the ball fly lower and usually further. If you're a beginner, you might want a driver with a higher loft to help you get the ball airborne.

The material of the driver is another factor to consider. Most modern drivers are made of titanium or composite materials. These light but strong materials allow you to swing faster and hit the ball further.

The shaft of the driver is just as important as the head. The shaft's length, flex, and material can all affect your swing. A longer shaft can increase your swing speed and be more challenging to control. Flex refers to how much the shaft bends during your swing. A more flexible shaft can add distance to your shots but might need to be more accurate.

The correct driver for you depends on your ability and style of play. Don't just choose a driver because it's the most expensive or because your favorite golfer uses it. Instead, focus on how the driver feels in your hands and how it performs when you swing it.

Getting a club fitting is an excellent way to find the right driver. A club fitting is a session with a golf professional who will measure your swing and recommend the best clubs. They'll consider your swing speed, ball flight, and physical attributes.

Getting a club fitting before purchasing is essential. It can save you from buying a driver that doesn't suit your game. Plus, a club fitting can also help you understand your swing better. It's a great way to learn about the mechanics of golf and how to improve your game.

Once you've chosen your driver, learn when and why to use it. A driver is usually used off the tee on long par-4 and par-5 holes. However, there might be times when another club, like a fairway wood or an iron, might be a better choice. Understanding when to use your driver is part of the learning strategy in golf.

The right driver can give you confidence on the tee and set you up for a good score. But remember, a driver is just one part of your golf game. Practice your swing, learn the rules, and enjoy the game. With the right driver in your bag and a love for the game, you'll be well on your way to becoming a great golfer.

Choosing the correct driver is more than picking the most expensive club. It's about finding a tool that fits your game and helps you play your best. So take your time, get fitted, and find the driver that's right for you. Remember, golf is a game of inches, and the right driver can make all the difference.

Techniques and Tips for Using a Driver

"Golf is a puzzle without an answer." - Gary Player

Golf is a game of precision, strategy, and skill. And at the heart of it all lies the most important tool in your arsenal: the driver. The driver is the longest club in your bag and has the lowest loft. It's designed to hit the ball the farthest distance, making it a powerful asset in any golf game. However, effectively wielding a driver is an enormous feat, especially for beginners.

The first technique to master with your driver is the grip. Hold the club lightly, with your hands positioned in a way that forms a "V" shape. The grip pressure should be firm but relaxed. Avoid gripping the driver too tightly, which can hinder your swing and reduce the club's effectiveness.

Understanding your stance is another crucial aspect of using a driver. Your feet should be shoulder-width apart, and your weight should be distributed evenly.

A slightly wider stance can add stability to your swing, allowing you to strike the ball with greater accuracy. Your body should be aligned with the target, and your ball position should be off your lead heel.

Swinging a driver is all about rhythm and timing. The backswing should be smooth and steady, setting the stage for a powerful downswing. The key here is to maintain a steady pace throughout the swing. Rushing your swing can result in a poor hit and decreased control over the ball's direction.

The point of impact is the most critical part of the swing. As you swing the driver, your goal should be to hit the ball on the upswing. This will help to maximize the loft and distance of your shot. Don't worry if you don't get it right the first time; mastering the driver takes practice.

A good follow-through is just as essential as the swing itself. After hitting the ball, your body should rotate naturally, and your weight should shift towards your lead foot. Your chest should face the target, and your club should be over your lead shoulder. A good follow-through ensures the ball travels in the desired direction and helps maintain balance.

Learning to control the driver is one thing, but understanding when to use it is another. The driver is most often used on the tee box for long par 4s and par 5s. However, the driver isn't always the best choice. Factors like the wind's direction and strength, the layout of the course, and the position of hazards can all influence whether you should use your driver or opt for a different club.

Club fitting is an essential part of golf that can drastically improve your game. A proper club fitting ensures your driver is tailored to your swing characteristics, including speed, launch angle, and spin rate. A well-fitted driver can lead to greater accuracy, distance, and consistency, making your time on the course more enjoyable and successful.

CHAPTER 5.

IRONS: ANATOMY OF AN IRON

The first part of an iron is the grip. This is where you hold the club. It's usually made of rubber or a similar material, designed to provide a comfortable and secure hold. The grip's size and shape can greatly influence your swing, so it's important to find a grip that fits your hand well.

Next is the shaft. This long, slender part of the club connects the grip to the head. It's typically made of steel or graphite. The shaft's length and flexibility can significantly affect your swing speed and the trajectory of your ball.

Then we come to the club head, the part of the iron that strikes the ball. The club head is composed of several parts. The face of the club head is the part that comes into contact with the ball. It's designed to be flat and smooth to ensure a clean strike. The face often includes grooves to help control the ball's spin and direction.

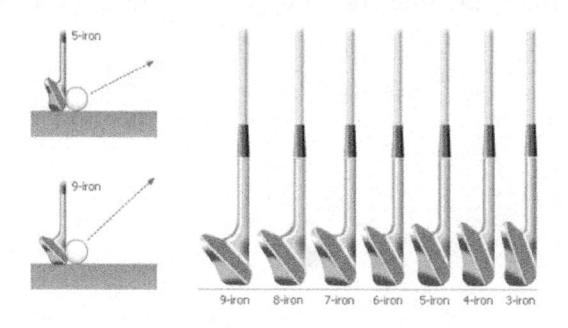

The back of the club head is called the back, which can be hollow or filled. This part of the club head can affect the club's weight distribution and help you control your swing. Then there's the sole, the bottom of the club head, resting on the ground. It's designed to glide smoothly over the grass, avoiding digging into the ground, which could affect your swing.

Lastly, there's the hosel, the part of the club head that connects to the shaft. It ensures a secure connection between the shaft and the club head. The hosel's angle can affect the club's loft, which is the angle at which the ball launches into the air.

Understanding the anatomy of a golf iron is crucial for beginners. It can help you appreciate the thought and design that goes into each club and guide you in choosing the right clubs for your game. Knowing how each part of the club affects your swing can also help you troubleshoot any issues with your game.

For instance, if you're having trouble getting the ball into the air, look at the loft of your club. If that's fine, you should examine the length and flexibility of your shaft. If you're having trouble controlling your swing, consider exploring the weight distribution of your club head.

Of course, understanding the anatomy of a golf iron is just one part of improving your golf game. Practice and experience are also crucial. But with a solid understanding of your tools, you'll be well-equipped to make the most of your practice and experience.

Types of Irons and Their Uses

"The value of routine; trusting your swing." - Larry Nelson

Golf, a game of precision and strategy, relies heavily on your clubs. So, let's talk about irons, a key element in any golfer's bag. Irons are used for various golf shots, from teeing off on shorter holes to making approach shots to the green. They're designed for precision, offering a range of options to suit every situation.

The most common types of irons are numbered one through nine, with the one-iron having the least loft and the nine-iron the most. The lower the number, the longer the iron, and the farther the ball will travel. But remember, lower-numbered irons are more challenging to hit well.

The one-iron, often called a 'butter knife' due to its thin appearance, is a difficult club to master. But when used correctly, it can send the ball soaring over long distances with a low trajectory. However, given its challenge, many players, especially beginners, opt to leave it out of their bag.

Two-irons and three-irons, also known as long irons, are handy for long fairway shots and can achieve a distance of up to 200 yards. They're helpful when you need to cover a lot of ground, but they're also tricky because of their low loft.

Four-irons and five-irons, or middle irons, strike a balance between distance and control. They're perfect for those mid-range shots where you need to carry the ball 150 to 170 yards. These clubs can be a beginner's best friend, offering a good mix of range and ease of use.

Six-irons, seven-irons, eight-irons, and nine-irons are classed as short irons. They're used for a shorter distance, more controlled shots, typically from 130 yards and in.

These irons have a higher loft, which helps lift the ball with a steeper trajectory, allowing for more precise placement on the green.

Another type of iron you should know about is the utility or hybrid iron. These clubs combine a wood's long distance and an iron's swing mechanics. Hybrids are an excellent option for beginners because they're easier to hit than traditional long irons and offer a better chance of getting the ball into the air.

Then there's the wedge, a specialized type of iron used for short, high shots to overcome obstacles like sand bunkers or tall grass. Wedges come in various forms, including the pitching wedge, sand wedge, gap wedge, and lob wedge. Each has a specific purpose and an array of uses around the green.

One key aspect to remember is that each type of iron requires a different swing style and stance. Learning how to adapt your swing to the club you're using is crucial. This is where practice becomes essential. Regular sessions at the driving range, focusing on different types of shots with each iron, can drastically improve your game.

Getting a proper club fitting before purchasing your irons is also critical. Golf clubs aren't one-size-fits-all. They should be tailored to your height, swing speed, and other aspects of your game. This ensures you can swing comfortably and effectively.

Choosing and Fitting Irons

"Golf is deceptively simple and endlessly complicated." - Arnold Palmer

When starting, you may be tempted to buy a set of top-of-the-line irons, thinking they will instantly improve your game. However, golf is a skill-based game, and having the most expensive clubs won't necessarily make you a better player. Instead, focus on finding clubs that suit your skill level and style of play.

One of the main things to consider when choosing irons is the clubhead design. There are three main types: blade, cavity back, and game improvement. More skilled players usually use blade irons because their thin, flat design allows more control. On the other hand, cavity back and game improvement irons have a more prominent sweet spot, making them more forgiving for beginners.

Next, let's address the topic of shafts. The shaft is the long, slender part of the club that connects the handle to the clubhead. Shafts can be made of steel or graphite. Steel shafts are heavier and more durable, while graphite shafts are lighter and can help increase swing speed. Graphite shafts are more suitable for beginners as they can help you get the ball airborne more easily.

Now, you've chosen your irons, but before you hit the checkout button, there's one more thing you need to consider - getting a proper club fitting. A club fitting is a process where a professional measures your swing speed, launch angle, and other factors to determine the best clubs for your game. Beginners often overlook this step, but it's crucial in ensuring that your clubs are suited to your swing.

Remember, golf is not a one-size-fits-all game. Just as each player has a unique swing, each player needs a unique set of clubs. Getting a proper club fitting ensures your clubs are tailored to your needs. This can significantly improve your game and make your time on the course more enjoyable.

Let's move on to using your irons. Knowing when and why to use particular clubs is essential to golf strategy. The lower the number on the iron, the longer the distance it can hit. A 3-iron, for example, can hit farther than a 9-iron. However, the higher the number, the higher the ball will fly, and the more it will stop on the green. Thus, you would use a 9-iron for a short shot where you want the ball to stop quickly and a 3-iron for a longer shot where distance is more crucial.

Techniques for Different Iron Shots

Iron clubs, known for their versatility, are your go-to clubs for a wide range of shots. They come in varieties ranging from 1-iron to 9-iron. The lower the number, the longer the shot you can make, and vice versa.

Understanding how to use each iron club is the first step in mastering your game. Let's dive into the techniques for different iron shots.

The 1-iron, or the driving iron, is often used for long shots from the tee or the fairway. To make the perfect shot with a 1-iron, position the ball towards your left heel and tilt your body slightly to the right. This posture will help you get the right swing and distance.

Next up is the 2-iron. This club is excellent for long fairways or tee shots on narrow holes. Its use is similar to the 1-iron, but remember to position the ball slightly further back in your stance.

The 3-iron and 4-iron, while less popular among beginners, can be powerful tools in your golfing arsenal. These clubs are typically used for shots around 200 yards from the hole. To swing these clubs, position the ball in the center of your stance and ensure your swing follows a straight path.

The 5-iron and 6-iron are great for mid-range distances. They are perfect for those tricky shots where you must cover distance and maintain control. To use these clubs, position the ball just forward of center in your stance.

The 7-iron, 8-iron, and 9-iron are typically used for shorter, more precise shots. These clubs are your best friends when you're close to the green and need to get the ball over a hazard or onto the putting surface. When using these clubs, position the ball in the middle of your stance and aim for a smooth, controlled swing.

Now that we've covered the basics let's discuss the shots you can execute with iron clubs.

Firstly, there's the standard shot, a straight and long shot ideal for fairways and greens. Then, we have the punch or knockdown shot, a low-flying shot used in windy conditions or to avoid overhead obstacles. Lastly, the lofted shot is perfect for getting over hazards or landing softly on the green. These shots require practice, but once you master them, your golf game will reach new heights.

Choosing the right club and mastering different shots is crucial in golf. But remember, golf is not just a physical but a mental game. As the legendary golfer Arnold Palmer once said, "Success in this game depends less on strength of body than strength of mind and character."

CHAPTER 6.

WEDGES: TYPES OF WEDGES AND THEIR USES

"The wedge is not just a club; it's your scalpel. It's your paintbrush." - Greg Norman

Understanding the types of wedges and their uses is crucial for a beginner golfer. The right wedge can significantly enhance your short game, often the key to lowering your scores. Let's start with defining what a wedge is in golf terms. A wedge is a subset of iron used for short distances, high altitude, and accurate utility shots. They are the game's workhorses, designed to perform specific tasks like lofting the ball high into the air or getting it out of tight spots.

There are four main types of wedges: pitching wedge, gap wedge, sand wedge, and lob wedge. Each of these wedges has a different purpose and degree of loft, affecting the distance and height of your shots.

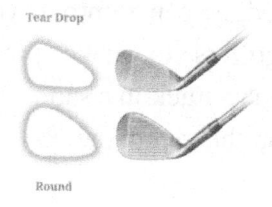

The pitching wedge is the most common type and is likely included in your standard club set. It's designed for longer approach shots, usually within 125 to 135 yards, and typically has a loft between 44 and 48 degrees.

Next, we have the gap wedge, sometimes called an approach or utility wedge. The gap wedge fills the "gap" between the pitching and sand wedge, hence its name. It typically has a loft between 50 and 54 degrees, making it suitable for shots that need more height and less distance than what a pitching wedge provides.

The sand wedge is designed for getting out of sand traps or bunkers. Its loft ranges between 54 and 58 degrees. It is characterized by a wider, heavier sole that allows the club to glide through the sand rather than dig into it. It's also practical for chip shots and pitch shots around the green.

The lob wedge is the youngest member of the wedge family. With a loft of between 60 and 64 degrees, it's the club you call on when you need to get the ball high into the air and stop it quickly on the green. It's beneficial for playing over hazards close to the green or for shots where the ball needs to stop quickly after landing.

Choosing the right wedge for a specific shot depends on various factors, including distance to the hole, the lie of the ball, wind speed and direction, and the obstacles you need to overcome. As a beginner, practicing with each type of wedge is suitable for understanding how they affect your shots and which situations call for each club.

The correct use of wedges can improve your game significantly. These clubs allow golfers to make precision shots in tricky situations. Whether you're stuck in a sand trap or trying to hit a high shot that lands softly on the green, there's a wedge designed for that purpose.

A good rule of thumb is to use the pitching wedge for longer approach shots, the gap wedge for shorter approach shots, the sand wedge for escaping bunkers, and the lob wedge for high shots that need to land softly.

Wedge Bounce and Grind

A golf wedge is a specialized club for short-distance, high-altitude, and high-accuracy shots. The term "bounce" refers to the angle between the leading edge of the club and the lowest point of the club's sole or the trailing edge. In simpler terms, it's the part of the club that bounces off the ground when you hit the ball. The bounce angle can vary from low (typically 4-6 degrees) to high (12-14 degrees). Your choice of bounce should depend on the course conditions and your swing style.

A high bounce angle is beneficial when playing in soft conditions or out of the sand because it prevents the club from digging too much into the ground. On the other hand, a low bounce angle is better for hard ground or tight lies because it allows the club's leading edge to get closer to the ball, making it easier to hit clean shots.

Now, let's move on to "grind." In the context of golf clubs, grind refers to manipulating the club's sole to alter its performance characteristics. Manufacturers modify or "grind" the club's sole in various ways to suit different playing styles and course conditions. For instance, a heel grind may benefit players who often open their clubface, as it allows the leading edge to remain low, enhancing control and precision.

Understanding the role of wedge bounce and grind can help you make informed decisions when selecting your clubs. Keep in mind that there is no "one size fits all" solution when it comes to golf equipment.

It's crucial to consider your swing characteristics, the typical course conditions you play in, and your comfort with the club.

For instance, a wedge with a high bounce and a wide sole may be beneficial if you have a steep swing and often play in soft conditions. Conversely, a low-bounce wedge with a narrow or standard sole could be your best bet if you have a shallow swing and play on firm ground.

When it comes to grind, you might prefer a club with heel and toe grind if you like to open your clubface for shots around the green. On the other hand, a full sole grind could be beneficial if you prefer a square face at impact.

Choosing the Right Wedge

"Golf is not, and never has been, a fair game." – Jack Nicklaus

Golf can be a challenging game, especially for beginners. One of the first steps to mastering it is understanding the equipment. Let's focus on one specific piece - the wedge. This type of club has a loft, and the angle of the club face is greater than that of a 9-iron. It's used for short-distance, high-altitude, and high-accuracy shots.

Choosing the right wedge depends on your playing style and the course conditions. There are four types of wedges: pitching, gap, sand, and lob. Each one serves a unique purpose in your golf game.

A pitching wedge is a versatile tool. It's mainly used for shots that need 110 to 125 yards and chip shots near the green. The average loft for a pitching wedge is between 45 and 50 degrees.

The gap wedge fills the 'gap' between the pitching wedge and the sand wedge. It typically has a loft between 50 and 55 degrees. It's used for shots that need to go 90 to 110 yards. It's also useful for chip shots and pitches.

Next, we have the sand wedge. As the name suggests, this wedge is designed to escape sand traps. It has a loft between 54 and 58 degrees. However, it's not limited to just sand traps. The sand wedge is also great for chip shots, pitches, and bunker shots.

Finally, there's the lob wedge. This wedge has the highest loft of 60 to 64 degrees. Its high loft can quickly get the ball high in the air, making it perfect for shots over obstacles. It's also useful for short-range shots that must stop quickly on the green.

But how do you know which one to choose when you're on the course? Here are some tips for shots that need to go over a short distance with a high arc, like over a sand trap or water hazard, using a lob wedge. A sand wedge is your best friend if you're in a sand trap or heavy rough and need to get the ball out. For medium-distance shots, go for a gap wedge when you need the ball to roll a bit. And for longer shots that need to get airborne and roll a bit once they land, use a pitching wedge.

Remember, the key to choosing the right wedge is understanding your needs on the course and your skill level. Starting with a pitching and sand wedge may be beneficial. You can add a gap and lob wedge to your bag as you get more comfortable with those.

Choosing the right wedge can make a significant difference in your game. It can help you navigate difficult shots and get closer to the pin. But remember, the best wedge in the world will only make a difference if you practice. So get out there and start swinging!

It's also important to have your clubs fitted to your swing. A proper fitting will ensure that your clubs match your swing speed and style, which can help improve your overall performance on the course.

Techniques for Effective Wedge Play

"The secret of golf is to turn three shots into two." – Bobby Jones

Short games often make a significant difference in your overall score in golf. That's where wedges play a crucial role. Wedges are designed to offer high loft, control, and accuracy, essential in short games. Most golfers carry at least two to three different types of wedges in their golf bag.

Understanding the value of wedges and the techniques to use them effectively can drastically improve your game. Wedges come in different types, including the pitching wedge, sand wedge, gap wedge, and lob wedge. Each of these wedges has a unique role and is used in different situations on the golf course.

The pitching wedge is the most common type of wedge. It has the lowest degree of loft, usually around 45 to 50 degrees. It's the wedge you'll likely use for shots that are too short for a full iron swing but too long for a chip. The pitching wedge balances distance and loft, making it a versatile club for many situations.

As the name suggests, the sand wedge is primarily used for bunker shots. It usually has a loft between 54 and 58 degrees. The sand wedge's unique design, with a wider sole and increased bounce, allows it to glide through the sand without digging too deeply, making it perfect for getting out of those tricky bunker situations.

The gap wedge, also known as an approach wedge, fills the "gap" between the pitching wedge and the sand wedge. It typically has a loft between 50 and 54 degrees. The gap wedge is perfect for those intermediate shots where a full swing with a pitching wedge might be too much, but more than a sand wedge is needed.

Finally, the lob wedge has the highest degree of loft, usually between 60 and 64 degrees. This club is used for short, high shots where you need the ball to stop quickly on the green. The lob wedge is perfect for hitting over hazards and getting out of deep rough.

Now that we've covered the types of wedges let's look at some techniques to maximize your wedge play. One of the most critical aspects of effective wedge play is control. This involves controlling both the distance and direction of your shots.

Practice is crucial to control your distance; spend time on the practice green, hitting wedge shots of different lengths. Start by making half swings with each wedge, then progress to three-quarter swings and full swings. This will help you understand how far each club can hit the ball with different swing lengths.

Directional control is equally important in wedge play. This involves both aiming your shots accurately and controlling the curve of your ball flight. Aiming is straightforward and can be improved with practice and alignment drills.

On the other hand, controlling the curve of your ball flight is a bit more complex. This involves understanding how the clubface interacts with the ball at impact. If the clubface is open, the ball will curve to the right; if it's closed, it will curve to the left. Strike the ball with a square clubface to hit straight shots.

CHAPTER 7.

PUTTERS: TYPES OF PUTTERS

"Golf is a game in which the ball lies poorly, and the players well." - Art Rosenbaum

The first type of putter we'll talk about is the blade putter. It's the most traditional type, with a narrow, flat design. Many golfers favor it because of its simplicity and the level of control it offers.

Next, we have mallet putters. They're larger, with a round, more substantial head. The extra weight can be beneficial since it helps to keep the putter stable during the stroke. This stability makes them a popular choice among beginners.

Then there are peripheral-weighted putters. These putters have additional weight on the edges of the putter head. This added weight can improve the putter's stability, which can be especially beneficial when dealing with longer putts.

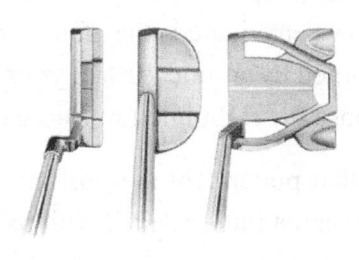

The center-shafted putter is another type to consider. In this design, the shaft attaches to the center of the putter head. This setup can give a different feel to the stroke, which some golfers prefer.

Belly putters are another option. They're longer than standard putters, with the extra length designed to be anchored against the golfer's belly. This anchoring can provide additional stability during the stroke.

Finally, we have the broomstick putter. It's the most extended type of putter, meant to be anchored against the golfer's chest. This design provides a very stable stroke, which can be helpful for those struggling with their putting.

As you can see, the variety of putter types is vast, each with unique advantages. The best way to determine which putter is right for you is to try them out. Spend some time at a golf shop or driving range where you can test different types of putters.

Furthermore, consider getting fitted for a putter. A proper fitting will consider factors such as your height and the length of your arms. This information can help you select the right putter for you.

Bear in mind that there is more than one-size-fits-all solution for putters. You might find that a specific type of putter works better for you than others. It's all about finding what feels comfortable and works best for your game.

Choosing the Right Putter

The putter is your final weapon on the golf course. It's your ticket to the hole after you've navigated the fairways and greens. Its importance is underlined by around 40% of your golf shots are putts. So, how do you choose the right one for your game?

Firstly, understand that putters come in different shapes and sizes. There are blade and mallet putters, each with its advantages.

Blade putters are traditional and offer better feedback, while mallet putters provide more stability. Your choice between the two comes down to personal preference and feel.

Next, consider the length of the putter. Standard putters are 34-35 inches long, but you can find them as short as 32 inches or as long as 52 inches. Your height, posture, and personal comfort play a role in determining the ideal length. An easy way to check if your putter is the correct length is to grip it and let your arms hang freely. If your eyes are over the ball, you're good to go.

The weight of the putter also matters. A heavier putter head provides more stability, especially on slower greens. Conversely, a lighter putter head is practical on faster greens. The weight can also influence the putter's feel and your control over it.

Then comes the putter's loft. Yes, even putters have loft. The standard loft of a putter is about 3-4 degrees. The loft helps lift the ball from any indentation made on the green and gets it rolling smoothly. A higher loft is beneficial if your hands lead the putter at impact.

The putter's grip is another important consideration. Putter grips come in various sizes and shapes, from thin and flat to thick and round. A larger grip can help reduce wrist action in your stroke, while a smaller grip might provide a better feel and feedback.

The balance point of the putter, determined by the design and weight distribution of the head, can affect how the putter aligns during your stroke. There are face-balanced putters, which have the face pointing upwards when balanced on your finger, and toe-balanced putters, where the toe of the putter points towards the ground. A face-balanced putter suits a straight back and straight-through stroke, while a toe-balanced putter is better for a stroke with an arc.

Fundamentals of Putting

Putting is more than just swinging a club. It's about precision, control, and understanding the game's terrain. The first thing to understand about putting is that it is a short stroke used to roll the ball into the hole. It's often used on the green and sometimes from just off the green when precision is more important than distance.

A proper putting stance is crucial. Stand with your feet shoulder-width apart, and hold the club with both hands. Your arms should hang down naturally, and your eyes should be over the ball. This stance allows for better control and accuracy.

Remember, the goal of putting is to get the ball in the hole with the fewest strokes possible. This requires understanding the green's layout, including its slopes and speed. Reading the green is a skill you'll develop with time and practice.

Your grip on the club is equally important. You don't want to hold the putter too tightly; a relaxed grip will give you more control and feel. There are various grips to choose from, and finding the one that feels the most comfortable for you is essential.

The stroke itself is another critical aspect of putting. Unlike a full swing, a putting stroke is more of a gentle rocking motion of the shoulders. Your hands and wrists should stay relatively quiet during the stroke.

Distance control is also a vital part of putting. You need to be able to judge how hard it is to hit the ball to get it to the hole. This can be influenced by factors such as the green's speed, the slope, and even the weather.

It would help if you also aimed your putts accurately. This can be challenging, involving lining up your putter correctly and reading the green.

It's also important to remember that the ball won't always roll straight - it can be influenced by the slope of the green and the grain of the grass.

Another critical point to remember is the importance of a pre-putt routine. A consistent routine before each putt can help calm nerves and ensure you're fully focused.

Lastly, always remember that practice makes perfect. The more you practice your putting, the better you will become. Spend time on the practice green, working on your stroke, distance control, and reading greens.

Advanced Putting Techniques

Golf is a game of inches. The smallest change can make the biggest difference.

It's true, especially when it comes to putting. Putting is a delicate, precise part of golf that can make or break your game. This section will explore advanced techniques to help you improve your putting skills.

Putting is not just about hitting the ball. It involves understanding the green, aiming your putts, and controlling your pace. The first advanced technique is understanding the green. Greens are not flat surfaces, and they have subtle slopes and undulations. To better understand the green, walk around the hole and look at it from different angles. It helps you visualize the path your ball will follow.

Aiming your putts is the next technique. Proper alignment is crucial in putting. Position your feet and shoulders parallel to your target line to improve your alignment. Use a practice stroke to aim your putt before actually hitting the ball. This practice stroke helps you visualize the ball's path and get a feel for the required pace.

Pace control is another advanced putting technique. To improve your pace control, practice different length putts. Start with shorter putts and gradually increase the length. The more you practice, the better you will become at judging the pace of your putts.

Another advanced technique is to maintain a steady grip pressure. A common mistake among golfers is to grip the putter too tightly during the stroke. It can cause the putter to move off-line, resulting in a missed putt. To avoid this, maintain a consistent grip pressure throughout your stroke.

The following technique is to keep your head still during your stroke. Moving your head can cause your body to move, throwing off your stroke. To keep your head still, focus on a spot on the ball and keep your eyes on that spot until after you have hit the ball.

Another technique is to use your shoulders to power your stroke. Your arms and wrists should remain passive during your stroke. Using your shoulders to power your stroke can make a smoother and more controlled stroke.

The final technique is to stay positive. Golf is a mental game; staying positive can help you perform better. If you miss a putt, don't get down on yourself. Instead, focus on what you can do to improve and keep practicing.

These advanced putting techniques can help you improve your game. However, they require practice to master. So, keep going if you see immediate results. Keep practicing, and you will see improvement over time.

CHAPTER 8.

HYBRIDS: ANATOMY OF A HYBRID

As the name suggests, a hybrid club is a fusion of two different types of golf clubs, the iron and the wood. They feature the wood's long-distance capabilities and the control and accuracy of irons. They're designed for versatility, and their unique construction lends itself to a wide range of uses on the golf course.

The head of a hybrid club showcases its dual nature. It retains the compact size and shape of an iron club head but borrows a wood club's rounded and slightly convex face. This design allows for power and control, making it ideal for those tricky long shots where precision is critical.

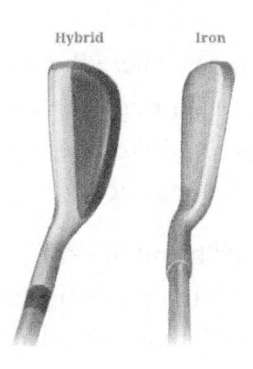

The center of gravity in a hybrid club is also a testament to its unique design. It's positioned low and to the back of the club, much like a wood. This feature aids in getting the ball airborne, making hybrids a popular choice for hitting off the fairway and even out of the rough.

The shaft of a hybrid club is another critical component. It's typically shorter than a wood but longer than an iron, striking a balance between control and distance. This intermediate length also makes it easier for beginners to handle, especially compared to the more daunting fairway woods.

Hybrid clubs are also famed for their forgiveness. If your swing isn't perfect or the ball doesn't hit the center of the clubface, a hybrid is more likely to correct your shot than other clubs. Their larger sweet spots provide more room for error, making them a beginner's best friend on the golf course.

Understanding the anatomy of a hybrid club is essential to maximizing its potential. But remember, it's not just about the club itself. It's also about when and how to use it.

For instance, hybrids excel in long par 3s and par 4s, where you need the distance of a wood but the control of an iron. They're also excellent for hitting out of the rough, thanks to their rounded heads and low centers of gravity. And for those tricky shots from the fairway, a hybrid can provide the confidence and control you need to reach the green.

But remember those instances where there might be better choices than a hybrid. In short, an iron might serve you better in par 3s or when you're close to the green. Likewise, a wood or driver might be more suitable for extremely long shots.

The beauty of golf lies in its blend of skill, strategy, and equipment. And the hybrid club, with its unique design and versatile nature, is a testament to this. It's a tool that can adapt to various situations, providing distance and control when needed.

But like any tool, its effectiveness depends on the craftsman. So before heading out to the course with your new hybrid, ensure you understand its anatomy and how to use it. Practice your swing, understand the club's strengths and weaknesses, and learn when to use it.

Having a hybrid in your bag can be a game-changer. But knowing how to use it properly can be the difference between a good shot and a great one. So, take the time to understand your hybrid and see how it can enhance your game.

When to Use a Hybrid

A hybrid is an excellent tool in your golf arsenal. It's a mix between a fairway wood and an iron, and it's designed to be easier to hit than a long iron. The club's design gives it a lower center of gravity, making it easier to get the ball airborne. Its wide sole also helps prevent the club from digging into the ground before impact, a common issue with long irons.

So, when is it ideal to use a hybrid? First, consider your distance from the green. A hybrid is perfect if you're too far for an iron but too close for a wood. The club offers a moderate distance with a higher trajectory than a fairway wood. It's also the ideal club when you're hitting from the rough. Why? The hybrid's design allows it to glide through the grass rather than getting caught up in it.

A common mistake beginners make is using a hybrid for long-distance shots only. However, it's much more than a substitute for your fairway woods or long irons. Its versatility allows you to use it in various situations, such as when aiming to cover a moderate distance from the rough, hitting from a tight lie, or even playing from a fairway bunker.

Let's discuss getting a proper club fitting before purchasing a hybrid. Club fitting is crucial because it ensures that the club you're using is tailored to your style of play. Factors like your swing speed, launch angle, and the golf course's conditions you usually play on should influence your chosen hybrid club.

Getting a club fitting is more manageable than it sounds. It involves a few tests with a professional who can guide you to the right clubs. The process considers your physical attributes, such as height, arm length, and swing traits. By getting a club fitting, you ensure you're using a club that complements your game, which is essential in a sport as nuanced as golf.

Choosing the Right Hybrid

Fore!

That's a term you'll hear quite often on the golf course. It's a warning shout to let people know a golf ball is coming their way. But today, we're not discussing errant shots but choosing the right hybrid golf club.

As you know, golf is a game of power and precision. The right club can make a major difference in your game. This is particularly true when it comes to hybrids.

Hybrids are a blend of the long irons and fairway woods. They borrow the best of both worlds. From the long irons, they take the ability to launch high and land soft. From the fairway woods, they take the design that makes it easier to hit the ball.

But how do you know which hybrid is right for you? The answer lies in understanding your own game and the specifics of the club.

First, consider your skill level. If you're new to golf, a hybrid with a larger head and more loft might be best. These can give you more distance and forgiveness on off-center shots.

Next, consider your swing speed. If you swing slower, a hybrid with more loft can help you get the ball in the air. For faster swingers, less loft might be better.

The correct shaft is also crucial. A lighter shaft can help increase swing speed, while a heavier one can offer more control. The flex of the shaft is also important. A stiffer shaft suits those with a fast-swing speed, while a more flexible shaft can benefit those with a slower pace.

The design of the hybrid can make a significant difference, too. Some hybrids have features like a low center of gravity to help launch the ball higher. Others might have a more compact design for better control.

But the most critical factor in choosing a hybrid is how it feels to you. When you swing the club, does it feel natural? Do you feel confident that you can hit a good shot? If the answer is yes, that might be your hybrid.

Remember, golf is a game of feel as much as skill. The right club can help enhance your natural abilities and make the game more enjoyable.

Before you buy, consider getting a club fitting to help ensure the club is the correct length, weight, and fit for your game. A proper fitting can make a significant difference in your performance.

Using the right club at the right time can also improve your game. For example, a hybrid is often a good choice when you're too far for an iron but too close for a wood. It can also be handy when you're in the rough or need to get over a hazard.

Lastly, remember to practice. Even the best club will only help if you know how to use it. Spend time at the driving range and on the course. Get to know your club and how it performs in different situations.

Hybrid Play Techniques

In the exciting world of golf, mastering hybrid play techniques is a game-changer. Hybrid clubs, a blend of irons and woods, offer a unique mix of distance and control. As a beginner, what's so special about hybrids? Why should I use them? You'll have those answers and more by the time you finish reading this section.

Hybrids offer the best of both worlds. They have the length and power of woods but the control and accuracy of irons. They're helpful in a range of situations on the golf course. When your ball is in the rough, a hybrid can cut through thick grass much better than a long iron. And when you're on the fairway, a hybrid can deliver the distance you need without sacrificing control.

Having a club fitting before purchasing your clubs is crucial. It ensures that the clubs you get match your physical attributes and swing characteristics. This way, you're not fighting against your equipment but working with it. A proper fitting can make the difference between a frustrating round and one of the best games of your life.

Remember, golf isn't just about power. It's also about precision. Knowing when and why to use specific clubs is key. Understanding the role of hybrid clubs can help. Hybrids can replace long irons or fairway woods in your bag, depending on your preference and playing style. For example, if you struggle with long irons, you might opt for a hybrid club to help you with those challenging shots.

How do you choose the right hybrid for you? Start by considering the distance you want to achieve. For example, if you're going to replace a 3-iron, you'll want a hybrid that can deliver a similar distance. But don't just focus on distance. Think about how the club feels in your hands. Is it comfortable? Do you feel confident when you swing it? These are essential factors to consider.

One of the most significant benefits of hybrid clubs is their versatility. You can use them off the tee, from the fairway, in the rough, and even for chipping around the green. This makes them a valuable asset for any golfer, especially beginners still developing their skills and understanding of the game.

Practicing with your hybrid clubs is essential. Like any other club in your bag, you need to get comfortable with your hybrids. Spend time at the driving range working on your swing. Pay attention to how the club feels and how the ball reacts when you hit it. Over time, you'll understand when to use your hybrids and what kind of shots you can achieve with them.

CHAPTER 9.

FINE-TUNING YOUR CLUBS

"Golf is a game of precision and consistency. The right tools make all the difference."

Getting a proper club fitting before purchasing your clubs can make a huge difference in your game. It ensures that your clubs are tailored to your needs and can improve your accuracy and distance. Additionally, it can help prevent injuries as you'll be using clubs designed for your specifications.

While club fitting is important, it's also essential to regularly assess your clubs' condition. Over time, the grips can wear out, or the clubface can become scratched or dented. Periodically checking your clubs for wear and tear can help ensure they're in the best possible condition for your game. If you notice any damage, immediately repairing or replacing your clubs is best.

In addition to checking your clubs' physical condition, you should consider how well they serve your game. If you're struggling with certain shots, it might be worth reassessing whether your current clubs are the right tools for your needs. For example, if you need help with long-distance shots, consider switching to a club with a larger clubface.

In golf, the most minor adjustments can make the most significant difference. This is especially true when it comes to your clubs.

You can significantly improve your game by regularly assessing their condition, getting them professionally fitted, and understanding their specific uses.

Remember that finding the clubs that best fit your style and needs is the goal. What works for one golfer may not necessarily work for you. So, take your time, research, and be bold and experiment until you find the perfect set of clubs for your game.

Enjoy the process as you fine-tune your clubs and improve your understanding of the game. After all, golf is a game meant to be enjoyed. So, whether on the fairway or practicing your swing at the driving range, always remember to have fun and enjoy the game.

The Benefits of Club Fitting

In the exciting game of golf, your equipment matters. As you're about to discover, club fitting plays a crucial role in your game. It's not just about buying the priciest set you can find. No, it's about finding the right fit for you - the clubs that match your swing, style, and aspirations.

Club fitting is a process you should consider to make your golfing life easier. It's an evaluation of your swing and other golf mechanics. Professionals use this data to recommend the right clubs for you. It's a game-changer and could be the secret sauce to improve your golf game.

Every golfer is unique with their swing and body dynamics. Your height, swing speed, and even how you grip the club all influence the clubs you should use. Club fitting takes these factors into account. The result? Clubs that feel like an extension of your body, enhancing your performance on the green.

Custom-fit clubs offer a level of comfort that boosts your confidence. When you know your clubs are tailored for you, you approach the tee with a different mindset.

Your swings are more precise, and your shots more powerful. You start to see improvements in your game, and most importantly, you enjoy playing more.

Investing in club fitting is investing in your golf future. It might seem unnecessary to some, but the benefits far outweigh the costs. It's about improving your game, but it's also about ensuring you enjoy every moment out on the course.

Club fitting can even prevent injuries. Too long or heavy clubs can lead to poor posture and strain. A proper fitting ensures you're using clubs suited to your body, reducing the risk of injuries and enhancing your overall golfing experience.

Now, how do you find the right club fitter? Look for professionals who are certified by reputable organizations. A good club fitter will take the time to understand your game, goals, and physical abilities. They will use this information to recommend the right clubs for you.

Club fitting is not a one-size-fits-all solution. It's a process that considers your unique golfing style and body mechanics. The clubs recommended for your friend may not fit you best. It's all about personalization, ensuring the clubs you use are perfect for you.

Golf is a game of precision and skill; your clubs play a significant role in your performance. The right clubs can enhance your swing, increase your distance, and improve your accuracy. Club fitting ensures you have the right tools in your golf bag tailored to you.

Club fitting is not just for the pros. Club fitting can enhance your game whether you're a beginner or an experienced golfer. It's about finding the right tools to match your unique swing and body mechanics. So, why not give it a try? Get your clubs fitted and see the difference it makes in your game.

Adjusting Lofts and Lies for Accuracy

When you're entering the world of golf as a beginner, you might think it's all about the swing. But there's a lot more to it. One overlooked aspect of the game is the adjustment of lofts and lies on your golf clubs. These two elements can significantly impact your game's accuracy and consistency. So, let's dive into the details.

First off, what are lofts and lies? In simple terms, the loft is the angle of the clubface that controls trajectory and affects distance. The lie is the angle between the center of the shaft and the ground line when the ground line is in a standard playing position. Now that we have that cleared up, let's discuss why beginners need to adjust these.

Adjusting the loft of your golf club can help you control the trajectory of your shots. A higher loft means a higher trajectory and can help you overcome obstacles on the course. It also results in a softer landing on the green, allowing for more precise control of your shot. On the other hand, a lower loft provides a lower trajectory, which is helpful for longer shots or when you're playing against the wind.

Then, we have the lie angle. This is crucial because if your club's lie angle is off, it can lead to inaccurate shots. You might send your ball off to the left if the lie is too upright. The ball might veer off to the right if it's too flat. Adjusting the lie angle to match your swing can significantly improve your shot's accuracy.

So, how do you adjust the lofts and lies of your golf clubs? It's not something you should try to do yourself as a beginner. Instead, it's best to get your clubs fitted by a professional. They have the tools and knowledge to adjust your clubs accurately.

They'll consider your height, swing speed, and other factors to ensure your clubs are perfect for you. You might be thinking, "But I'm just a beginner.

Is it really necessary for me to get my clubs fitted?" The answer is a resounding yes. Even as a beginner, having clubs that are fitted to your specifics can improve your game significantly. It can help you develop good habits and avoid the frustrations of consistently inaccurate shots.

However, it's also essential to understand that adjusting your lofts and lies isn't a one-time thing. As you improve and your swing changes, you should get your clubs adjusted again. Regular checks are an excellent idea to ensure your clubs are still suited to your game.

After all, golf is a game of precision. The most minor details can have the most significant impact on your game. And when it comes to accuracy, adjusting the lofts and lies of your golf clubs is a detail you can't afford to overlook.

When and Why You Might Need to Re-Grip

"Golf is the closest game to the game we call life. You get bad breaks from good shots; you get good breaks from bad shots - but you have to play the ball where it lies." - Bobby Jones

To truly embrace the spirit of golf, the connection between you and your club must feel natural, almost instinctive. The grip on your golf club facilitates this connection. The grip is your primary point of contact with the club, and it plays a crucial role in how well you can control your shots.

Over time, the grip of your golf club can wear out. This is a normal part of the progression as you play more and more golf. The key signs that your grip is wearing thin include:

- Visible wear and tear.
- A lack of tackiness to the touch.
- Slipping in your hands during swings.

It's important to understand that a worn-out grip can drastically affect your game. A slippery grip might increase grip pressure, causing tension in your hands and arms, ultimately leading to poor shot results.

The frequency of re-gripping is contingent on how often you play. For an avid golfer who plays weekly, re-gripping should ideally be done once or twice a year. But the frequency can be adjusted accordingly if you're starting and playing less often.

It's essential to remember that re-gripping isn't just about maintenance. It's also an opportunity to customize your club to your preferences and playing style. Grips come in various styles, sizes, textures, and materials, each with advantages.

For instance, a larger grip can help players with larger hands or those with arthritis, as it eases the strain on the hands and wrists. On the other hand, smaller grips are suitable for players with smaller hands or those who prefer a more precise feel of the club in their hands.

Texture plays a role in comfort and control. Grips with many textures, such as corded grips, provide excellent traction and are ideal for players who sweat or play in wet conditions. Smooth grips, meanwhile, are softer and can be more comfortable for some players.

Material is another important factor. Rubber is the most common material used because of its durability and variety. However, other materials like leather, thermoplastic rubber, or high-tech polymers are also available. These materials can provide different levels of softness, tackiness, and durability.

Re-gripping your clubs is also a chance to experiment with different colors and designs. While this may not directly affect your performance, it can enhance your enjoyment of the game. After all, golf is as much a mental game as a physical one.

Re-gripping is a minor aspect of golf but can significantly impact your game. A fresh, well-suited grip can improve your control over the club, enhance your swing, and even help prevent injuries. It's a simple and cost-effective way to improve your performance and enjoyment of the game.

So, pay attention to the importance of your golf club's grip. Check your grips regularly for signs of wear and tear. When the time comes, don't hesitate to re-grip. Remember, golf is a game of details, and every detail counts.

Remember Bobby Jones' words as you continue to learn and grow in the game of golf. Play the game as it is, not as you wish it to be. Adapt, adjust, and always strive to improve. And sometimes, that improvement can start with something as simple as a fresh grip on your club.

CHAPTER 10.

GOLF CLUB MAINTENANCE

"Golf is a game of respect and sportsmanship; we have to respect its traditions and its rules." - Jack Nicklaus.

This quote by one of golf's greatest players sets the tone for our discussion on golf club maintenance. As a golfer, respecting the game and your equipment is crucial.

Your golf clubs are your partners on the course. Keeping them in peak condition can make a significant difference in your performance. Just like a car needs regular servicing, golf clubs need regular maintenance. This chapter will guide you through all the necessary steps to ensure your clubs are always ready for the next round.

Regular cleaning is the first step in golf club maintenance. Dirt and debris on your clubface can affect your shots. Clean your clubs after every round with warm water and a soft brush. Dry them thoroughly to avoid rust. Always remember to check your club heads for any signs of damage. Dents or cracks can affect your swing and the flight of the ball.

The grips on your clubs are equally important. They provide the connection between you and your club. Over time, grips can become worn and lose their tackiness, resulting in the club slipping during your swing. Regularly inspect your grips for wear and replace them as needed.

Golf club shafts are the backbone of your clubs. They determine the flex and control of your swings. Regular inspection of your shafts is crucial to maintain their optimum performance. Look for any signs of bending or cracking. If you notice any issues, it's best to have them checked by a professional.

Storing your golf clubs is another essential aspect of club maintenance. Never leave your clubs in the trunk of your car. The heat and humidity can warp the shafts and damage the grips. Store your clubs in a cool, dry place. A golf bag with individual dividers can provide extra protection for your clubs.

Golf club maintenance also involves regular check-ups by a professional. Just as you would take your car to a mechanic, bring your golf clubs to a professional for an inspection at least once a year. They can spot any potential issues and provide expert advice on how to keep your clubs in top shape.

Cleaning Routines for Different Clubs

Golf is deceptively simple and endlessly complicated bemoaned Arnold Palmer, one of the greatest golfers ever. The same could be said about golf clubs, the heart and soul of any golfer's game. The cleanliness of your golf clubs might seem minor, but it can significantly impact your performance. Let's dive into the cleaning routines for different clubs.

A clean club allows better contact with the ball, improving your control and accuracy. It's like having a clean slate, a fresh start. This is particularly true for the grooves on your golf clubs. These small indentations on the clubface help generate spin and control the ball's flight path. You're unlikely to make consistent, quality shots if these are dirt-filled.

So, how do you clean your golf clubs? The process is simple. You'll need a bucket of warm, soapy water, a toothbrush, and a towel. Start by soaking your clubs in the water for a few minutes. This helps to loosen any stubborn dirt on the clubface.

Next, take your toothbrush and gently scrub the clubface, ensuring you get into all the grooves. Remember to clean the back of the clubhead and the grip. Once you're done cleaning, rinse the club under a tap to remove any remaining soap. Lastly, dry your club thoroughly with a towel.

The process for cleaning woods and irons is the same. However, the materials used in these clubs differ, leading to slight variations in the cleaning routine. Woods, particularly modern ones, often have a painted finish. Therefore, you should avoid using any abrasive materials when cleaning them.

Irons, on the other hand, are more durable and can withstand a bit more scrubbing. However, it's essential to stay focused. Scrubbing too hard can damage the grooves, reducing their effectiveness.

Putter cleaning is also crucial, though it often gets overlooked. A clean putter ensures your ball rolls smoothly on the greens, increasing your chances of sinking those crucial putts. The cleaning process is the same as for other clubs. However, you should pay particular attention to the putter's face, as this is the part of the club that comes into direct contact with the ball.

Beyond regular cleaning, taking care of your clubs is also important. Store them in a cool, dry place when they're not in use. Avoid leaving them in your car; the heat can damage the glue holding the clubhead and shaft together.

Maintaining your golf clubs is about more than cleanliness. It's about ensuring that your equipment is in the best possible condition so that you can perform at your best. It's about respecting the game and the tools of your trade.

Proper Storage Tips for Longevity

The right set of clubs in golf is as essential as the golfer's skill set. As a beginner, you have invested in clubs that will take your game to the next level. It's not just about choosing the right clubs but also about taking care of them. Proper storage of your golf clubs ensures they serve you for a long time.

Golf clubs are an investment; you want to get the maximum value for your money. Proper storage is one way to ensure this. It involves cleaning your clubs after each round, storing them in a dry place, and protecting them from harsh weather conditions.

After a game, make sure to clean your clubs. Dirt and moisture can cause damage to the clubface and shaft. A quick wipe with a damp cloth and thorough drying can prevent this. Remember, the goal is to keep them looking new and ensure they perform their best.

Storing your clubs in a dry place is essential. Moisture can lead to rust, which can affect the performance of your clubs. If you store your clubs in a garage or basement, ensure the place is dry and that the clubs are not in direct contact with the ground. Elevating your golf bag off the floor can prevent moisture damage.

Temperature regulation is essential for golf club storage. Extreme temperatures, either hot or cold, can damage your golf clubs. The glue that holds the club head and shaft together can weaken under extreme temperatures.

A golf club cover is a worthy investment for your clubs. It provides extra protection against dust, moisture, and scratches. Be sure to cover your clubs when not in use. It is also a good idea to periodically check your clubs for any signs of damage.

If you travel with your clubs, consider investing in a hard case for transportation. It will provide extra protection against knocks and bumps that could damage your clubs.

Proper storage of your golf clubs can extend their life and ensure they perform well. It can also save you money in the long run. You will have to replace your clubs less often, allowing you to invest that money in other areas of your game.

Remember, your golf clubs are an extension of your golf game. Treat them with care, and they will serve you well. Just like Arnold Palmer said, success in golf involves character. Part of that character is treating your equipment with respect.

Checking for Wear and Tear

"You can't expect to hit the jackpot if you don't put a few nickels in the machine." - Flip Wilson

As you delve into the world of golf, one aspect that needs your attention is the wear and tear on your golf clubs. Like any sports equipment, golf clubs are not immune to the ravages of time and use. Regular usage, environmental factors, and how you store them can contribute to gradually wearing down your clubs. This wear and tear affects the aesthetic appeal of your clubs and can significantly impact your performance on the course.

Golf clubs are your tools of the trade in this game. A painter's brushes or a chef's knives must be maintained in top condition for optimal performance. If a club is worn out or damaged, it can affect the accuracy and distance of your shots. Even a slight change in the club's weight distribution or a small dent on its surface can throw off your swing, leading to less-than-desirable results on the golf course.

Understanding the signs of wear and tear on your golf clubs is essential for every golfer, especially beginners. This knowledge lets you address any issues before they negatively affect your game. Some common signs of wear include scratches or dents on the clubhead, a worn-out grip, and a bent or damaged shaft.

The clubhead is one of the most critical components of your golf club and the part that undergoes the most stress. It's exposed to impact with the golf ball and the ground, leading to potential damage. Look out for scratches, dents, or changes in the clubhead's surface. These imperfections can affect the club's performance, disrupting the airflow around the club during your swing, leading to less accurate shots.

The grip on your golf club is another area you need to monitor. A worn-out grip can cause the club to slip out of your hands during your swing. Look for any signs of wear, such as the material's fading, hardening, or cracking. A good grip should feel comfortable in your hands and provide a secure hold during your swing.

The shaft of your golf club can also suffer from wear and tear. Check for any bending or damage. A bent shaft can affect the trajectory of your shots, and any substantial damage could even lead to the shaft breaking mid-swing. Ensure that the shaft is straight and free from significant dents or scratches.

Another aspect to consider is the wear and tear on your golf clubs due to improper storage. If you store your clubs in a damp or humid environment, it can lead to rusting. Similarly, storing them in a place with extreme temperatures can cause the materials to expand and contract, leading to potential damage. Always keep your golf clubs in a dry, temperate environment to prolong their lifespan.

While it's essential to check for wear and tear, knowing how to address these issues is equally important. If you notice any damage, don't panic. Many minor issues can be fixed with a bit of care and maintenance. For example, a worn-out grip can be replaced relatively easily. Suppose the damage is more severe, such as a bent shaft or a significantly dented clubhead. In that case, it might be worth considering getting a new club.

CHAPTER 11.

THE ART OF THE SWING

The art of the swing in golf is a thing of beauty. It's a balance of power and precision, a blend of skill and instinct. Mastering this art is one of the most rewarding parts of the game, but it can also be challenging. It's about more than swinging as hard as you can. It's about understanding the mechanics of the swing, learning how to control your body, and using the right club for the right shot.

One of the first things to understand about the golf swing is its complex motion. It involves a series of coordinated movements that must be executed in the correct sequence. Think of it as a chain of events. Each link in the chain has a specific role, and if one link is out of sync, the whole chain can fall apart.

The swing starts with the setup. This is where you position yourself in relation to the ball. Your feet should be shoulder-width apart, your knees slightly bent, and your spine straight but tilted forward from the hips. Your arms should hang naturally from your shoulders, with your hands gripping the club.

From the setup, the swing moves into the takeaway. This is the initial movement of the club away from the ball.

The takeaway should be smooth and controlled, with the club moving back along a path parallel to the target line. The clubface should remain square to the target for as long as possible.

The next phase of the swing is the backswing. This is where you rotate your body and lift the club to the top of the swing. The backswing should be a fluid motion, with your body rotating around your spine. The club should reach the top of the swing in a position parallel to the ground and pointing towards the target.

From the top of the swing, you move into the downswing. This is where you start to transfer your weight from your back foot to your front foot. As you do this, you should rotate your body towards the target and begin to bring the club down towards the ball. The downswing should mirror the backswing, with the club moving along the same path but in the opposite direction.

The impact is the moment of truth in the golf swing. This is where the club makes contact with the ball. Your body should be in a strong, balanced position at impact, with your weight primarily on your front foot. The clubface should be square to the target, and the ball should be struck with the center of the clubface.

The swing ends with the follow-through. This is where you complete the rotation of your body and bring the club up to a finish position. The follow-through is a sign of a good swing. If you can hold your finish position until the ball lands, it's a good indication that you've made a solid, balanced swing.

The swing is the heart of golf. It's the action that sends the ball towards the target. But it's not just about the swing. It's also about the club. Different clubs are designed for different types of shots. The driver is made for distance. The irons are made for precision. The wedges are made for control. And the putter is made for finesse.

The driver is the longest club in the bag, and it's used for the longest shots. The driver is designed to hit the ball off the tee and send it as far down the fairway as possible. The driver has a large, rounded head and a long, flexible shaft.

The large head gives the driver a big sweet spot, making it more forgiving on off-center hits. The long shaft allows you to generate a lot of clubhead speed, which translates into distance.

The irons are used for various shots, from long approaches to short chips. The irons have a flat, angled face that allows you to control the trajectory and spin of the ball. The lower-numbered irons (like the 3-iron and 4-iron) have less loft and are used for longer shots. The higher-numbered irons (like the 8-iron and 9-iron) have more loft and are used for shorter shots.

The wedges are used for short, high shots around the green. The wedges have a high degree of loft, which allows you to lift the ball high in the air and land it softly on the green. The wedges also have a wide, flat sole, which helps to prevent the club from digging into the ground on short shots.

The putter is for rolling the ball along the green and into the hole. The putter has a flat face and a short, stiff shaft. The flat face helps to keep the ball on line, and the short shaft gives you better control over the speed of the putt.

In golf, the swing and the club go hand in hand. You can only have one with the other. Mastering the art of the swing means learning how to use the right club for the right shot. It means understanding the swing's mechanics and the club's characteristics. It's a journey of discovery, a process of learning and improvement. And it's one of the most rewarding parts of the game.

Fundamentals of a Good Golf Swing

"The most important shot in golf is the next one." – Ben Hogan

The game of golf is a blend of skill, strategy, and a touch of luck. At its heart, though, lies the swing. A good golf swing is a work of art, a perfect blend of power, precision, and timing. For beginners, mastering the golf swing can seem a daunting task. But don't worry. We will break it down and make it simple for you.

Golf swings are dynamic. They involve the whole body and not just your arms. Your legs, torso, and head play crucial roles in a good swing. The trick is to ensure all these parts work in sync. You'll quickly find the ball flying off to your target when they do.

The first step towards a good swing is the grip. Your hands are the only contact point with the club; hence, the grip is vital. Hold the club in your palms and wrap your fingers around it. Ensure your grip is firm but tight enough. A tight grip could cause your swing to be off balance.

Next is the stance. Stand with your feet shoulder-width apart. Your weight should be evenly distributed between your feet. The ball should be in line with the inside of your lead foot. This stance provides a stable base and allows for a full range of motion in your swing.

Once you have a good grip and stance, focus on the backswing. This is the part where you lift the club away from the ball. Keep your eye on the ball as you do this. Your body should rotate as you lift the club, pulling your lead shoulder towards the target. This rotation is what provides the power for the swing.

The next phase is the downswing. This is where you bring the club down to hit the ball. The power comes from your hips and torso, not your arms. As you swing the club down, your body should uncoil, releasing the power stored during the backswing.

The moment of impact is crucial. You want to hit the ball at the center of the clubface. To do this, keep your eye on the ball and maintain a steady head. At this point, your body should be square to the target, and your arms fully extended.

Then comes the follow-through. This is the part of the swing after the ball has been hit. The club should naturally continue to move upwards and around your body. Your body should turn towards the target, and your weight should shift onto your front foot.

A good golf swing is about more than just the mechanics. The right mindset is also needed. Golf is a game of patience and focus. Be calm and composed, especially under pressure. This mental strength can differentiate between a good swing and a great one.

Role of Different Clubs in Swing Mechanics

"Golf is about how well you accept, respond to, and score with your misses much more so than it is a game of your perfect shots." - Dr. Bob Rotella

Your driver, or the 1-wood, is the club that will give you the most distance. It's typically used for your first shot on a par-4 or par-5 hole. The driver has a large head and shaft, which allows you to swing with more force. This means a longer shot but less control.

The fairway woods are numbered 3, 5, and 7. They're used after the driver when you're still far from the green but need more precision. These clubs have a smaller head than the driver and slightly shorter shafts. They give you a balance between distance and control.

Your irons are numbered 1 through 9, with 1 being the least used and 9 the most. The lower the number, the less loft and more distance you get. These clubs are used for various shots, from the fairway to rough or bunker. They're the workhorse of your golf bag, used in many different situations.

Hybrid clubs are a cross between woods and irons and are used instead of long irons, which are harder to hit. They're great for beginners because they combine wood's easy-to-hit nature with irons' accuracy.

Wedges are used for short approach shots into the green, chip, pitch, and bunker shots. They have the highest loft of any club, which gives you a high, short shot that can stop quickly on the green.

The putter is used for rolling the ball into the hole once you're on the green. It has a flat face to keep the ball on the ground. Putters come in various shapes and sizes, but they all have the same purpose: to give you precise control over your shot.

Each club has a unique role in your swing mechanics. The driver's long shaft and large head allow you to swing hard and fast for maximum distance. With their flat faces and shorter shafts, the irons encourage a more controlled swing for precision shots. The wedges' high loft lets you swing under the ball, creating a high, arching shot that lands softly on the green.

The swing mechanics also change with each club. Your driver swing should be a sweeping motion, while your iron shots require a descending blow. Slide the club under the ball for your wedge shots.

Understanding these differences can help you choose the right club for each situation. Remember, golf is not just about power. It's also about strategy and making the right choices. Knowing the role of each club in your bag and how to use them will help you improve your game.

Golf club fitting can also play a crucial role in your game. A proper club fitting can ensure that your clubs match your swing style, body type, and skill level. This can greatly improve your performance on the course.

Tips to Synchronize Your Swing with Your Clubs

When you hold a golf club, feel its weight, the grip, and the shaft length. These factors will influence how you swing and the golf ball's trajectory. A heavier club requires more force but can also give you more control. So, choosing a club that suits your physical strength and swing style is essential.

It's not about swinging as hard as you can. It's about swinging smart. A well-synchronized swing will allow the club to do most of the work. When your swing is in harmony with your club, you will find it easier to hit the ball accurately and consistently.

To synchronize your swing, you need to understand the rhythm of your swing. This is the sequence of movements from the start of your swing to the follow-through. A good rhythm allows for a controlled and smooth swing, which, in turn, enhances your ability to hit the ball accurately.

Club fitting is an essential step in golfing. This process tailors the club to your specific needs and abilities. A club with the right fit will make it easier to swing consistently and accurately. It will also help prevent injuries from swinging a club unsuited to your body or swing style.

Using the correct club for a particular shot is another way to synchronize your swing with your club. For example, a driver is ideal for long-distance shots, such as the tee shot on a par 5. On the other hand, an iron is more suited for shorter, more controlled shots, like those needed to get out of a bunker or onto the green.

The more you play, the more you understand which club to use for different situations. This understanding comes from experience and practice. So, don't be discouraged if you don't get it right the first time. Keep practicing, and you will get better.

Fairway Woods can be a great asset in your golf bag. These clubs are designed for long-distance shots, particularly those taken from the fairway. They have a larger head than irons, which makes them more forgiving, especially for beginners. Their design also makes hitting the ball high and far more manageable, which can be a significant advantage on long par 4s and 5s.

Remember, golf is a game of precision, not power. It's not about how hard you can hit the ball but how accurately you can hit it. This is where the synchronization of your swing with your clubs comes into play.

Your swing reflects your understanding of the game, physical abilities, and mental approach. It's a complex mix of mechanics, physics, and psychology. So, take the time to understand your swing and clubs and how they interact. This understanding will help you to synchronize your swing with your clubs, improve your game, and enjoy golf more.

CHAPTER 12.

MASTERING THE SHORT GAME

Golf is a game of inches. The closer you get to the hole, the more those inches matter.

The short game in golf is about precision. It's about getting the ball close to the hole, or better yet, in the hole, with just one swing. It's the part of the game that makes a good golfer great. Mastering the short game should be a top priority to improve your overall golf game.

When you watch a professional golf game, you will notice one thing: their short game is impeccable. They can get the ball to stop, turn, and even spin on command. And it's not by luck; it's through practice and understanding the science behind each shot.

The short game involves various golf clubs, but the most common are the putter and wedges. These clubs have a high loft, meaning they can raise the ball quickly and land softly. This is crucial when you are near the green and need the ball to stop quickly.

The putter is your best friend when it comes to the short game. It's the club you will use when you are on the green and taking a shot at the hole. Unlike other clubs, the putter has a flat face, which helps keep the ball on the ground and rolling towards the hole.

One thing to remember when using the putter is to keep your stroke smooth and steady. A common mistake beginners make is hitting the ball too hard, causing it to roll past the hole. Remember, the aim is to get the ball into the hole, not beyond it.

Conversely, Wedges are used when you are close to the green but not on it. They are designed to get the ball high in the air and land it softly on the green. There are different types of wedges, each designed for a specific situation. For instance, you have the pitching wedge for long chip shots, the sand wedge for getting out of bunkers, and the lob wedge for high and short shots.

When using a wedge, the key is to control your swing. Unlike with the driver, where you want to hit the ball as far as possible, with the wedge, it's all about control. You want to hit the ball just right so it lands softly on the green and rolls towards the hole.

Club fitting is an essential part of mastering the short game. Each golfer is unique, and so are their clubs. The length, weight, and the club's grip should match your physical attributes and playing style. This is why getting a club fitting before purchasing your golf clubs is recommended. It ensures that the clubs you use are perfect for you, making it easier to master the short game.

Practice is the final piece of the puzzle. The short game is not something you master overnight. It requires hours of practice and a lot of patience. But the more you practice, the better you get. Before you know it, you'll sink putts and make chip shots like a pro.

It's a funny thing, the more I practice, the luckier I get. - Gary Player

The Importance of Wedges in Your Short Game

Getting caught up in the driver's power or the putter's precision is easy. But there's a set of clubs that often gets overlooked by beginners, yet they're essential to mastering the game. I'm talking about wedges. The short game, which includes shots played on or near the green, is where many games are won or lost, and wedges are the key players in this part of the game.

Why are wedges so vital? Well, they're designed for precision. Their high lofts and specialized designs allow for various shots around the green. From sand traps to thick rough, a good wedge can help you escape tricky situations and set up easier putts. With practice and the proper technique, you can use a wedge to hit the ball high and stop it quickly on the green, giving you more control over where it lands.

Now, there are several types of wedges, each with its purpose. The pitching wedge, for instance, is excellent for longer shots into the green or chip shots. It typically has a loft between 45 and 50 degrees, making it less lofty than other wedges but still more than most irons. As the name suggests, a sand wedge is designed for getting out of sand traps. It has a loft between 54 and 58 degrees and a wider sole that helps it slide through the sand without digging in.

Then, we have the gap wedge and the lob wedge. A gap wedge fills the "gap" in the loft between a pitching wedge and a sand wedge, typically with a loft between 50 and 54 degrees. This versatility makes it a handy club to have in your bag. On the other hand, a lob wedge has the highest loft of any club, usually between 58 and 64 degrees. This club can send the ball high into the air and land it softly on the green, making it perfect for shots over obstacles or when you need the ball to stop quickly.

But more than knowing about the different types of wedges is required. Learn when to use them and how to swing them properly. Understanding that a wedge isn't just a shorter version of a full swing is crucial. The technique involves a more wristy action and less body rotation. It would help if you also considered factors like the ball's lie, the distance to the hole, and the conditions of the green when choosing which wedge to use and how to play the shot.

Remember to consider the importance of practice, too. Even the pros spend hours working on their short game. It might not be as thrilling as smashing a drive down the fairway, but mastering the wedge can save you a lot of strokes and frustration on the course. To get started, try setting up different scenarios around the practice green and use your wedges to solve them. See how the ball behaves with different clubs, swings, and lies. This will help you better understand how to use your wedges effectively.

Chipping, Pitching, and Bunker Play Techniques

Chipping, pitching, and bunker play are integral parts of golf. These techniques are not just about the clubs you use but also about your approach, mindset, and the execution of the shot. Let's delve into these techniques, providing you with the skills you need to improve your game.

Chipping is a fundamental skill that beginners often overlook. It's a shot used around the green when you want the ball to spend more time on the ground than in the air. Use a less lofted club like a 7 or 8 iron to execute a chip shot. Position the ball back in your stance and take a narrow stance with your feet closer together. The swing should be more like a putt with minimal wrist action, relying more on the shoulders to do the work.

A pitch shot is played more through the air, not having as much roll. This technique is used when you need the ball to travel more in the air than on the ground. It's a high shot over a short distance, usually within 50 yards of the green. A pitch shot is performed with a highly lofted club, often a pitching or sand wedge. The ball should be placed in the middle of your stance, and your weight should favor your front foot slightly. Unlike chipping, the swing is like a mini full swing, with a wrist hinge on the backswing and a follow-through.

Bunker play, or sand play, is another crucial skill. It can be pretty intimidating for beginners, but with the proper technique, it can be mastered. The objective of a bunker shot is not to hit the ball first but the sand under the ball. It's one of the few golf shots where you aim to avoid striking the ball directly. The club of choice is a sand wedge due to its bounce and loft. Aim to enter the sand about two inches behind the ball and follow through as if trying to splash the sand onto the green.

Each of these techniques requires practice. More than just merely reading about them or understanding them is necessary. You must get out there on the green and put these techniques into practice. The more you practice, the more comfortable you will become, and the better your game will be.

Remember, golf is as much about strategy as it is about skill. Knowing when to use a chip, pitch, or bunker shot is as important as knowing how to execute them. It is about understanding the golf course and the situation and making intelligent decisions.

Putting: Choosing the Right Putter and Mastering the Stroke

As a beginner in golf, the first step is understanding the game's tools. The putter, an essential club in your bag, is your golden ticket to mastering the green. The putter's role in your game cannot be overstated. It's used more frequently than any other club and is pivotal to your overall score.

Choosing the right putter is a mix of personal comfort and scientific principles. When selecting a putter, pay attention to its length, loft, and lie. These factors can drastically improve your putting performance when correctly aligned with your posture and stroke style.

Consider the putter's length first. When you stand in your natural, comfortable putting posture, the putter's length should allow your eyes to be directly over the ball. Longer putters can help stabilize your stroke, while shorter ones offer more control.

Next, look at the putter's loft. This is the angle of the putter face relative to the vertical. The correct loft helps the ball start on its intended line, reducing the chances of skidding or bouncing. Standard putter lofts range from 2 to 4 degrees, which can be adjusted to suit your stroke style and the green conditions.

The putter's lie is another critical factor. This refers to the angle between the shaft and the ground when the putter is in its address position. The correct lie angle ensures the putter's sole sits flat on the ground, promoting a square strike at impact.

Once you've found the right putter, you need to master the art of the stroke. The key to a good putting stroke is consistency. You want to repeat the same motion every time, ensuring the ball travels the intended distance and direction.

The grip is a crucial part of your putting stroke. While there are several grip styles, the most common are the reverse overlap, cross-handed, and the claw. Each has its advantages and suits different types of players. Experiment with these to find what feels most comfortable and allows you to control the putter face.

Your stance and alignment are also critical. Aim to have your feet shoulder-width apart and parallel to your target line. Your eyes should be over the ball, and your arms should hang naturally from your shoulders. This setup promotes a smooth, pendulum-like stroke.

The stroke itself should be a simple back-and-forth motion driven by the shoulders. Avoid using your wrists or hands, as this introduces unnecessary variables and makes consistency harder to achieve. The power should come from the size of your shoulder turn, not the speed of it.

CHAPTER 13.

IMPROVING YOUR GAME

※

"Success in this game depends less on strength of body than strength of mind and character." - Arnold Palmer.

Welcome to an exciting part of your golf journey. We're talking about improving your game. It's time to take those clubs and swing them with more confidence, accuracy, and power. This chapter will guide you on how to do just that.

Golf is a sport that requires patience and practice. And being a beginner, it's critical to take it step by step. Your first few rounds can be quite challenging. But with the right mindset and approach, you can steadily progress and enjoy the game even more.

Choosing the right club can significantly impact your performance. Fairway Woods, for instance, are versatile clubs that can help you cover great distances. They are convenient when you're too far to use an iron but too close for a driver. Knowing when to use these clubs is vital to improving your game.

Proper club fitting before purchasing is also an essential consideration. Clubs that are too long, short, heavy, or light can all hinder your swing. A club fitting will ensure that your clubs match your height, swing speed, and other physical characteristics. This reduces the risk of injuries and promotes an efficient swing.

Using the right club at the right time can be a game-changer in golf. Each club in your bag has a specific purpose and is designed for certain situations. For instance, drivers are used for long-distance shots, typically off the tee, while putters are used for short, precise strokes on the green. Learning these nuances can significantly enhance your performance.

You should notice some common pitfalls as you continue to hone your skills. One such mistake is trying to hit the ball too hard. A smooth, controlled swing often yields better results than a powerful, hasty one. It's more about technique and timing than brute strength.

Another common mistake is neglecting the short game. Many beginners focus too much on driving and neglect their putting and chipping. Remember, golf is a game of precision, and every stroke counts. Spend time practicing your short game, and you'll see a marked improvement in your overall score.

Golf is also a mental game. Staying calm under pressure, maintaining focus, and managing your emotions are all vital to your performance on the field. Remember, even professional golfers miss shots. The key is to learn from your mistakes and move on.

Don't be afraid to seek help, either. Hiring a coach or taking lessons can provide valuable insights into your swing and overall game. They can offer tailored advice and corrections you might not notice alone. Plus, they can provide mental strategies to help you handle the pressures of the game.

In addition to practice and coaching, watching others is another effective way to improve. Pay attention to skilled players—both in person and on television. Notice their posture, their swing, their strategy. You can learn a lot from observing their techniques and tactics.

Practice Routines and Drills

"The more I practice, the luckier I get." - Gary Player

For a beginner golfer, these words from a golf legend may sound simple. But they hold a wealth of wisdom. Golf isn't just about hitting the ball. It's about precision, control, and consistency. And these come with practice. Let's focus on some essential practice routines and drills to help you improve your game.

The first routine you need to master is the grip. A good grip forms the foundation of a solid golf swing. Grab a club and practice holding it in different ways. The perfect grip is when the club rests in the base of your fingers, with your thumbs pointing down the shaft. Hold the club firm, but don't squeeze too hard. Repeat this until it becomes second nature.

Next, work on your stance. Your feet should be shoulder-width apart, with your weight evenly distributed between them. Your knees should be slightly bent, and your spine should be straight. This posture gives you the stability you need for a good swing. Practice standing this way each time you pick up a club.

The swing is the most complex part of golf. It's a fluid movement that requires coordination of your entire body. Start by swinging without a ball. Focus on moving smoothly from your backswing to your downswing. The idea is to create a rhythm. Once you're comfortable, add a ball and practice hitting it.

Practicing putting is also essential. Putting requires a different grip and stance from the swing. The grip should be softer and the stance more relaxed. Practice aiming at a target and hitting the ball with just enough force to reach it. The key here is to control the speed and direction of the ball.

Chipping is another skill you need to develop. It's used when you're close to the green but not close enough to putt. The goal is to loft the ball onto the green and let it roll towards the hole. Practice this by setting targets at different distances and trying to hit them.

Bunker shots can be tricky for beginners. But with practice, you can turn this challenge into an opportunity. The trick is to hit the sand, not the ball. Practice this by drawing a line in the sand and trying to hit it out using a sand wedge.

Driving range sessions are a great way to practice your swing and gain distance. But don't just aimlessly hit balls; set goals for each session. Try to hit a certain number of balls within a specific area or aim for a particular distance.

Using Technology to Analyze and Improve Your Game

The game of golf, as Arnold Palmer so aptly put it, is as much about mental agility as it is about physical prowess. As a beginner golfer, you might find the myriad of factors to consider daunting. There's a lot to take in, from the type of clubs to use, the stance to adopt, the swing style to perfect, and understanding the course itself. But fret not; technology is here to help simplify things and accelerate your learning curve.

In sports, technology has become an invaluable tool for performance improvement. In golf, this is no different. There are numerous golf technologies available that can help you understand your game better and make necessary improvements. From golf simulators to swing analyzers, these technologies provide instant feedback and detailed data that you wouldn't be able to get from just practicing on the course.

A golf simulator is an advanced technology that uses sensors and software to replicate the experience of playing golf in a virtual setting. While it can only partially replace the experience of playing on an actual course, it provides an excellent platform for practice and analysis. It measures your swing speed, ball speed, launch angle, and spin rates. With this data, you can clearly understand where you need to improve.

Swing analyzers, however, are more focused on improving your swing. They use sensors attached to your club or body to measure various aspects of your swing. This includes the club's speed, the angle of the club at impact, the path of the swing, and more. Again, this data provides a clear picture of your swing and helps pinpoint areas that need improvement.

Besides these tools, there are also mobile apps designed to help golfers. Apps like 'Golfshot' or 'Hole19' offer GPS rangefinder features, digital scorecards, and statistical tracking. They can help you understand the course better and keep track of your progress over time.

You might wonder how one uses this data to improve their game. The key lies in understanding what these metrics mean and how they affect your game.

Swing speed, for example, refers to how fast your club moves at the point of impact. It's a crucial factor in determining how far the ball will go. If your swing speed is slow, you should work on your strength and flexibility to increase it.

Launch angle, on the other hand, refers to the angle at which the ball leaves the clubface. A higher launch angle means the ball will fly higher and potentially further. However, it's not as simple as 'higher is better.' The optimal launch angle depends on your swing speed and your club.

Understanding these metrics and how they relate is essential in improving your game. With this understanding, you can make targeted improvements, whether adjusting your swing, changing your stance, or selecting a different club.

The Importance of Consistent Play with Your Set of Clubs

Let's set the stage. You've just begun your exciting journey into the world of golf. You've got your shiny new clubs, and you're raring to go. But wait, there's an essential factor you need to consider - consistency. Why is it necessary, you ask? Let's dive into it.

Consistency is the key to progress in any sport, and golf is no exception. It's all about repetition and muscle memory. The more you swing your club, the better you'll get at it. There's a lot of science behind this. According to a study by the University of Southern California, muscle memory is critical in learning and mastering sports skills.

In golf, muscle memory helps you swing the same way every time. It enables you to maintain the exact grip, the same stance, and the same follow-through. So, when you continuously use the same set of clubs, your muscles get used to them. They get used to the weight, the length, and the feel of the clubs. This consistency can significantly improve your accuracy and performance.

Now, imagine switching your clubs often. Each club has a different weight, a different length, and a different feel. This could confuse your muscles and disrupt muscle memory, leading to inconsistent swings and poor performance.

Moreover, using the same set of clubs allows you to understand them better. Each club has its unique characteristics. Some are suited for long shots, some for short ones.

Some are ideal for a swing with a steep angle, while others work best with a shallow angle. The more you use a club, the better you understand its nuances.

By sticking to the same club set, you also know which club to use in which situation. For example, you'd know that the driver is best for long, straight shots from the tee, while the wedge is ideal for short, high shots that must stop quickly. This understanding can be a game-changer on the golf course.

Consistency also applies to club fitting. According to a National Library of Medicine study, club fitting can significantly improve a golfer's performance. When you get your clubs professionally fitted, they are tailored to your body and swing. This means they are the perfect length for you, have the right grip size, and have the proper shaft flex. They are, in essence, an extension of your body.

Now, with your custom-fitted clubs, you're ready to dive into the game. But remember, golf is not just about the clubs. It's about strategy, precision, and patience. It's about understanding the course, the wind, and the weather. It's about making the right decisions at the right time.

And it's about practice. Lots and lots of practice. Because no matter how great your clubs are, they can't do the work for you. Ultimately, you have to swing them. You need to master them. And for that, you need consistency.

Congrats! Note from Rico Fairway:

You've reached the end of the book!

Thank you for finishing Golf Clubs for Beginners: Selecting, Using, and Improving Your Clubs!

Looks like you enjoyed it!

If so, would you mind taking 30 seconds to leave a quick review on Amazon?

We worked hard to bring you books that you enjoy!

Plus, it helps authors like us produce more books like this in the future!

Here's where to go to leave a review now:

https://amzn.to/49dHtrE

Customer reviews

⭐⭐⭐⭐⭐ 4.8 out of 5

399 global ratings

5 star	▇▇▇▇▇▇▇▇▇	88%
4 star	▇	9%
3 star		2%
2 star		1%
1 star		1%

˅ How are ratings calculated?

Review this product

Share your thoughts with other customers

> Write a customer review

111

Made in the USA
Monee, IL
13 April 2025